Grief
50 Questions *and* Answers

peeling back the layers

Grief
50 Questions *and* Answers
peeling back the layers

Award Winning Author
Richard Ballo, BS, MBA

Grief 50 Questions and Answers
Peeling back the layers

Printed in the United States

Published by
Tolman Main Press
2670 Horseshoe Dr. N., Suite #203, Naples, FL 34104
239-263-0214
www.tolmanmainpress.com, www.Richardballo.com

Names: Ballo, Richard, author.
Title: Grief, 50 questions and answers: peeling back the layers / Richard Ballo, BS, MBA.
Description: Naples, FL: Tolman Main Press, [2021] | Includes bibliographical references and index.

Identifiers: ISBN 9781945518072 (softcover)

Subjects: LCSH: Grief--Miscellanea. | Death--Psychological aspects--Miscellanea. Personal belongings--Psychological aspects--Miscellanea. | Dating (Social customs) --Miscellanea. | Questions and answers. | LCGFT: FAQs

Classification: LCC BF575.G7 B35 2021 | DDC 155.937--dc23

Neither the publisher nor the author is engaged in rendering professional advice or services to the individual reader. All matters regarding your physical and mental health require professional and medical supervision.

Editorial Services: Bookbaby.com, Cover design: Christine Dupre,
Interior design: Jessica Angerstein

Dedication

This book is dedicated to my parents, the late Stephen and Rose Ballo. They showed me how to be in peace when faced with a terminal illness, how to be compassionate, and for letting me be there in their final days to give them the love, compassion, and caring they passed on to me. Miss you always.

Table of Contents

Acknowledgements i

Preface iii

Introduction 1

Anger: Why am I so angry? 5

Anniversaries: How do I survive anniversaries? 9

Bed: When is a bed more than a piece of furniture? 13

Blended Families: How do I blend families? 17

Cemetery: How often do I visit the cemetery? 21

Children: How do I talk to children about death? 25

Coping: How do I cope after the death of a loved one? 31

Counseling: Does grief counseling really work? 35

Dating: Do I have to date? 39

Death and dying: What are the universal realities of death and dying? 49

Doing it all: What to do when your spouse did it all? 53

Dreams: Why do I dream of the dead? 57

Escaping: Can I escape grief? 61

Father's Day: How do I celebrate Father's Day? 65

Firsts: What are the first 365? 69

Forgetting: What is stuck between remembering and forgetting? 73

Friends: What about our friends? 77

Giving in or up: What is giving up or giving in? 81

Going home: What is going home? 85

Grief attacks: What is a grief attack? 89

Grieving: Do I have the strength to grieve? 93

Grieving: How long do I grieve? 97

Guilt: Why do I feel guilty when I did nothing wrong? 103

Holidays: How can I make it through the holidays? 105

Hope: When does hope die and return? 109
Hospice: Can hospice help the living? 111
Hurtful words: What words hurt a person in grief? 115
Intimacy: Can I be intimate again? 117
Journaling: How can journaling help? 123
Living: What is living again? 127
Memorials: What type of memorial should I have? 131
Memories: How do I create new and happy memories? 135
Memories: When to share memories? 141
Mother's Day: How do I celebrate without the kid's mom around? 145
New spouse: How do I relate to a new spouse? 149
Overwhelmed: Why am I easily overwhelmed? 153
Personal items: How do I separate from personal items? 157
Photographs: How photographs can hurt or help? 163
Questions: Why did they die? 167
Rings: What about our rings? 171
Sex: Can I have sex again? 177
Sharing widowhood: Who do I share widowhood with? 181
Single parent: How do I parent as a widower? 185
Spiritual: Do we still have a connection with the deceased? 191
Stages of grief: Do I have to go through them? 195
Stress: How can stress affect my physical health? 199
Valentine's Day: How do I feel good? 203
Visiting the past: Do I have to visit the past? 207
Watching a death: What is it like watching someone die? 211
We to Me: How do I move from 'we' to 'me'? 215
Epilogue 221
About the Author 223
Other books by Richard Ballo 225
References 227
Excerpt from 360 Degrees of Grief 234

Acknowledgements

I would like to thank my friend Jane, and my mother-in-law Roberta, for sharing their stories about grief and loss for this book.

I am also grateful to the many men and women who write and offer services and healing for grief issues. They can be found on the web and they are referenced in the endnotes.

I would like to thank the editors at Bookbaby for the great job they did in correcting my mistakes. Also, thanks to designers Christine Dupre and Jessica Angerstein for the great designs to make the book look great.

Also, to the men and woman who let me into their lives when their loved ones died or were dying, and let me sit by the dying person's bed. It is a profound experience and thank you for letting me be there.

I would like to thank my wife, Terri, who put up with me during the writing of this book, and for patiently editing this book too. I thank her for being by my side so I can enjoy marriage and family life again.

Preface

You are going to be okay.

Really, you are going to be okay.

I did not hear these words after my wife died, and I wanted to hear them. I wanted to be assured that I was going to be okay, because it did not feel like I was ever going to be okay again.

Grieving is a messy business. It is complicated, emotionally agonizing as it comes with feelings of hurt, anger, self-doubt, and most of all, uncertainty. This is because it is usually the first time that we face such strong, hurtful emotions brought on by the death of someone we love.

But it is going to be okay.

How do I know this?

Because I have lived through it.

I was 39, when my 38-year-old wife died of cancer. We had two biological sons, and a foster daughter we were going to adopt. I did not adopt our foster daughter, and so I suffered that loss as well. Years later, I had a girlfriend that was killed in a motorcycle accident, and I had a broken engagement. All my buttons have been pushed, all sorts of wounds and feelings opened.

But I am okay.

I, and many others, have worked through grief, and we are okay. Grief did not feel the same for each loss, and I did not react the same way, because I was a different person at the time of each event. I had grown and grieved before, and I am okay. I even wound up at the point where I remarried because I could see the future, and I heard it in the things that I said and the way I acted around her. And it is not just okay—it is great.

Great because I waited, and I could see and accept that person in my life, and I wanted a life with that person. More importantly, I could accept who I was and where I was.

Each relationship, each person, opens a door in our life to learn, love, grieve, and then move on with more experience than before. Experience teaches you that being open to what happens and seeing the right moment in time when you know you have moved past grief and are ready for whatever comes next.

You will be okay.

Introduction

Thank you for choosing *Grief 50 Question and Answers* to learn about grief issues that revolve around the death of a loved one. This book is a compilation of questions that I have asked myself and that others have asked me. Some of these questions and answers have appeared on my website, richardballo.com, or have been answered on other websites. Any loss, be it divorce, loss of a job, pet, or loss of a body part, comes with grief. In this book, I refer to the loss of a loved one.

I use the terms spouse, partner, wife, loved one, passed, passed on, died, and deceased interchangeably to refer to the person in my life, and your life, who died.

This book does not have to be read in order. The reader can pick and choose the topic that appeals to them. Each story stands on its own. Some essays refer to other parts of the book, but the main point will not be lost by reading the essays in any order you want.

Some answers were written with the raw emotion of early grief, while others have been written with the passage of time that allowed me to reflect and examine the subject.

I write about grief not to relive grief, because that would be a painful way to live. I write about grief to show my errors, gained knowledge, and adaption as a way for you to learn from my experience.

There is a lot to learn about grief and the human response. My responses have fascinated me, and I find that what I went though is like what others have gone through, but they have not spoken about it. That is why I explore it and write about it. I want you to know that grief affects a person on many levels and all those levels need to heal. We need to restore ourselves and become the people we used to be, so we can go on living in the present.

I lived 20 years as a widower before I found the right woman to marry. I learned a lot in the preceding years, and in my new marriage, about grief, about myself, my reaction to grief and how that has affected my life.

Each person is different, and our grief is different because it depends on the relationship we had with the deceased. I know widowers who remarried a year after losing a spouse. Some never remarry. Young or old, man or woman, we go through the same range of emotions and face many similar issues.

Does grief end?

Yes and no.

The 'in your face grief' of the initial loss fades into the background as life goes on. Grief is an emotion like joy, happiness, anger, or jealousy. It is tied to a memory. It is in our memory for the most part, and it is silent unless something triggers a memory of grief.

Grief changes us. It is an experience that adds to our life and our perspective.

I hope that the information and insights in this book help you on your journey to understanding grief issues.

Remember that you are not alone. We all have losses. We all grieve, and we will all be okay.

Richard Ballo, 2021

Anger

Why am I so angry?

Anger is an emotion that sometimes has no words, says the American Psychological Association in an article on anger. Anger is a completely normal, usually healthy, human emotion. But when it gets out of control and turns destructive, it can lead to problems—problems at work, in your personal relationships, and in the overall quality of your life. And it can make you feel as though you are at the mercy of an unpredictable and powerful emotion.

"Why didn't you tell me?" I yelled to an image I have of Lisa in my mind. She died 6 months ago.

"Why did you leave me like this, with three kids? Why did you leave when I needed you the most?" I wipe at the tears.

"You could have talked to me," I whisper, as the anger dissipates.

I was angry.

After Lisa died, I was angry at anything and everything. It seemed so irrational.

I was angry that snow and ice backed up on the roof of our New England house and caused water to drip into the living room just hours before we were to fly back home to Florida.

I was angry at Lisa for not talking to me and telling me how sick she was. I was angry at her for leaving me. I was angry at people who did not acknowledge my loss. I was angry at myself and at God. Being angry at God is normal.

I was angry.

"It's perfectly normal to be angry," says Dr. Diana Jacks, a retired clinical psychologist with a specialty in grief counseling and those who had experienced a tragic loss. She adds, "You can't convince them (widows) not to be angry, but you can encourage the person in mourning to find healthy ways to vent their anger—such as punching a pillow, running, or writing a letter and burning it."

Jane, a colleague of my wife and a widow, was angry at her late husband too. She said she was angry "at him for not being truthful when he said he wouldn't leave me," she said. Fortunately, the episodes of anger she felt have subsided as the years went on.

Why was I angry? Why is anyone angry at losing a loved one?

I was angry because my wife was taken from me at a young age. It was unfair to take a mother from her children. It was unfair to take away the woman I loved after only 8 years of marriage. Lisa and I married when we were in our early thirties, and eight years later, she was dead.

Why?

I don't know the answer, but I hope to find out on the other side of life.

As Dr. Jacks said, being angry is normal. According to the American Psychological Association (APA) article 'Controlling anger before it controls you', you need to give yourself a break. Make sure you have some "personal time" scheduled for times of the day that you know are particularly stressful.

I found the following healthy ways to vent my anger.

Exercise. Nothing burns off more energy than physical exertion. You can go to a gym, swim, walk, run, or bicycle. I would jump on my bike and pedal as hard as I could until my energy and anger dissolved.

Yes, I was angry because the relationship I had, and the person I had it with, had been cut short, and there wasn't anything I could do to fix it.

You can also pound a rock. Get a rubber mallet and a rock, and then bang the rock with the mallet. It may help to also yell at the rock and tell it why you are angry. This can be done at any time inside or outside the home.

Write an angry letter. Write a letter to whoever you are angry at and then burn the letter or tear it to shreds. It gets the hurt emotions out and gives you a physical release through action.

Start a remodeling project. This is like pounding a rock but on a bigger scale. Nothing feels better than taking a sledgehammer to a wall and breaking the plaster board.

Throw plates. Buy some old plates and find a safe place to smash them. You can just throw them or use a hammer.

Each of these actions should be accompanied by verbalizing what you are angry at. It is both a physical and emotional release of pent-up anger. It is a safe way to vent and will help relieve you of your anger.

When you get angry, be assured that it is a normal response to your loss. It is an expression of your grief. Let your anger out in constructive ways. Anger will lessen as time goes on.

Anniversaries

How do I survive anniversaries?

Anniversaries come in many varieties. There are birthdays, death days, wedding days, divorce days, and days where we remember presidents and entertainers. Some are public days and others are private.

Each anniversary brings with it the emotions of joys or sadness, expectation, or regret. The emotions are neither good nor bad. "Emotions that have to do with loss are triggered throughout our lives, and you will live with them. Usually they are in the form of anniversary reactions," said Mary C. Lamia, Ph.D., in Psychology Today.

My wife died just 10 days before Christmas. Her birthday was in January, mine in February, and our wedding anniversary in March. I was hit with my major anniversary days within 75 days of her death.

I dreaded each anniversary. When I thought of them, I did not know how I would react to the memories and emotions that were associated with that day. The actual day was not as traumatic as I thought it would be, and that was a relief. I discovered that the days leading up to the anniversary were far worse than the actual day.

Yes, anniversaries can trigger grief reactions years after the traumatic event. Even if we have dealt with the emotion, it is still with us.

"Grief is an emotion that sends a vague alert to help you to remember, rather than to forget," said Dr. Lamia.

To remember? Yes, to remember.

I did not want to remember my grief, but I wanted to remember my wife who died. In remembering, we have the chance to move away from grief and see the good in that anniversary. As each anniversary came, I worked through the emotions associated with each anniversary, and was able to grieve less and remember the good moments more.

This was an important step in my grief work. I had a sense of healing and coming to grips with the past. Healing brings a recognition of that day, good feelings, and acceptance.

But reactions to grief anniversaries can vary from calm to abusive according to the website Griefcounseling.org. People can be withdrawn, reflective, or unorganized. Some may turn to drugs, alcohol, or sex, to avoid the holiday feelings.

You must accept that setbacks happen said the website Grief Healing, and that they are normal. Handle your memories with care; plan for those anniversary days. You can also let people know that you will be having a bad day and have them nearby to help you.

If you have children, like I had, then the preparation for anniversaries takes on more importance. I wanted the children to have good memories of their mother, so I had to have good memories of her to tell them. The stories of their time with their mother were important to their emotional well-being. They needed the reinforcement that their mother wanted them, loved them, and didn't want to leave them.

So I would pull out pictures of our anniversary days, and tell them stories of that day, like the day before our wedding when grandpa fell and broke his ankle. But he was determined to walk their mother down the aisle and did so using crutches.

On your anniversary, whichever one you celebrate, create a tradition that is for you and your children, if you have them. Remember the day and why it was important. Pull out pictures, letters, or other memorabilia that you may have to remember the event. If you have good memories, talk about them. Encourage others to share as well.

In this electronic age, many people share anniversaries on Facebook. Not only birthdays and weddings, but death anniversaries as well. It is not something I did or do now. I can see why people post the death of someone they love when that person dies, but I have a hard time accepting the post if the person has been dead ten years or more. It is not my way of remembering the date. In my opinion, it is an anchor to the past. I would have to remember the day they died as a conscious event in my mind, and then share it. I do not want to share that anniversary. I was there. I know it happened. I do not want people giving me sympathy or pity after so many years. Each person must deal with the dates differently. Sharing on Facebook is not what I do. Many on Facebook didn't even know her.

On the anniversary of her death I may call friends and reminisce about that day and what it meant to us, and how we are doing today. My friends remember that day and what it means to them, each in their individual way.

Each year is different as you move away from your loved one's death. I am 26 years away from her day of death. The exact day has no hold over me anymore. I remember her in my heart. The other days, her birthday, our wedding day, are just days now. Sometimes I remember the day after it has passed. Why? Because it was a generation ago since she died. I have new anniversaries to remember and celebrate with the living.

When you have anniversaries coming up, remember that day in a way that is unique to you. It depends on the relation, the time since the event happened, and where you are today. In any case, be gentle with yourself. And when you meet others who have their anniversary dates, let them take the lead about their loved ones. There are good memories there. If you forget the date, don't be hard on yourself. It happens. Life happens as we live each day, and some anniversaries do not have to be observed.

Bed

When is a bed more than a piece of furniture?

I never thought much about beds besides looking forward to the comfort of the bed at the end of the day. As a young adult, I had a foam mattress that I carried from apartment to apartment. The mattress sat on the floor or on a support base.

By the time Lisa and I married, she had moved back home because her mother died and she wanted to help her dad and not leave him alone. In discussing where to live, and the fact that Lisa didn't want to leave her dad alone, it made more sense for me to move in with them, than have Lisa and I move to an apartment or house, and have her father live alone. I had lived with my parents for the past five years and living with a parent was nothing strange for me.

The bed we slept in was an antique sleigh bed with a lumpy, antique, horsehair mattress. The frame was loose and creaky. I shoved some old paperback book pages into the loose spaces of the rails to stop the creaks. In that bed and on that lumpy, old mattress, my wife and I made babies, talked, cried, held each other, and rubbed each other's backs. We had our favorite sides. She was to my left. Sometimes we would switch sides too, just for fun.

For 7 and half years, we slept together in that bed, until my wife's declining health forced her into a hospital for care. I still slept on my side of the bed, keeping her side unused until she returned.

The hospital's bed had side rails and the bed could move and reposition her, and there was a call button and the TV remote at the ready. The kids, our sons, 6 and 5, liked to sit in the bed and move it up and down. Kids. So easy to please at that age.

I slept in the old bed, on my side, waiting for her to return.

She never returned to reclaim her side of the bed.

Then the entire bed was mine. I could sleep on either side or right in the middle. There was no sharing, except when the kids jumped up on the bed.

After Lisa died, I moved over and slept on her side. I don't know why I did this, but I did. It gave me some comfort, and I just accepted that that was all there was to it.

During a grief support group meeting at my local hospice, they asked us what side of the bed we slept on. Apparently, it is common for the surviving spouse to sleep on their mate's side so we wouldn't have to see their side of the bed empty.

That is where I found myself. I was on her side of the bed so that I would not see her side of the bed unoccupied. It was occupied but by me. It is a trick our mind plays to help us cope with the loss.

Being on our spouse's side of the bed takes away a reminder that they are gone. There are so many reminders that they are gone, but we can take away this one.

After a period of grieving, I decided it was time for a change. I ordered a new mattress and box spring instead of using that old, lumpy mattress. The new mattress was firm and higher than the old one, but it was more comfortable. The bed still creaked when I sat on it.

As time when on and life changed. I bought a new bed frame and mattress. I disassembled the old bed, and my grown sons and I loaded it onto a truck and moved it a couple of hundred miles to a vacation house we had. The bed was still good, and I did not want to give it away or throw it away. It still had function and value.

I reassembled the old bed using new wood screws on the base and wood shim by the rails to stop the creaking noises. It was the same old bed but in a new location, and yet it had been improved a bit and still gave me a good night's sleep.

I used the bed in the vacation house for many years. I hoped that one day, when and if I remarried, that my wife would like the bed. If she didn't, then it would be an antique that someone else could use.

I rented the vacation house out, and it was four years later that I saw the bed again.

It was still a good piece of furniture, and I knew my new wife and I would not sleep in it.

I sold the vacation house, and we bought a new vacation condo in a converted mill building that was closer to our families. I had to clean out the old vacation house because the new owners didn't want the bed and most of the other furniture. I could have thrown the old bed out or sold it. But I did neither. My practical side took over. I have a hard time throwing away good stuff. Yes, I was attached to that old bed. I did not hate it or grieve over what it meant or represented. It was an antique.

We moved it, along with tables, chairs, and lamps, to our vacation condo. We sleep in a new bed with an old style to it.

The old bed fits in with the style of the old mill building and we set it up it in the guest bedroom. The old creaky frame has been fixed. The mattress is still good and provides our guests with a place to sleep, and they have no emotional attachment to the bed. To them it is just a bed.

It is an old bed that is still useful. I remember the times we, then I, slept on it, but time passes, and now it is just a classic, antique bed that others use, and it matches the rest of the furniture. I have accepted that it is just a piece of furniture. Maybe I am attached to it as I still have it.

What to do with an old bed? I kept mine in use instead of spending money. My guests like it. You are the one to decide what the bed means—is it a memory trigger or just a place to sleep? What gives you comfort is what matters.

Blended Families

How do I blend families?

A blended family is when you remarry after a divorce or the loss of a loved one, and the person you are marrying has children, or you are the one that has the children, or you both have children.

How do I blend my family into a new marriage, or enter a marriage where a widow or widower may have other kids?

"When you remarry and take your children into a new family, the choices you make and the perspective you live with will have even more of a compound effect than if you were entering marriage without children on either side," said Sean Cort, author and ordained minister, in Psychology Today.

I was faced with the blended family prospect after my wife died. Most of the women I met, who were in my age range of 35-40, were married with children, or divorced with children, or never married and had no children.

The single moms and divorced moms were the ones I dated. They had children. I was looking at the prospect of a blended family. It was a good thing that I liked kids.

Multiple sources point to the fact that about 65% of remarriages will involve children. I was in that statistical group. Blended families can run into problems with the children from one parent not respecting the new parent. Amy Gunn, a graduate student, wrote a research paper at the University of Wisconsin- Platteville, on counseling successful blended families, recommends open communication. Communications between parents, and parents and children is essential so that everyone knows what the rules are in discipline, responsibility, and power.

My kids wanted to be the only kids in the family, just like they were. Sometimes at school, they were teased because their dad was dating Mrs. So-and-so. There were many divorced women in my age range. It was awkward dating parents of my kids' friends when they were in middle school. It became easier as they went to high school because I didn't know their new friends. The women I dated generally didn't have kids that my kids knew.

It can be a problem when getting into a blended family where the kids are the same age and attending the same school. Kids can be cruel to each other. You need to talk to your kids about this before it happens.

When my current wife Terri and I were dating, we stayed at my house. Her daughter was a senior in high school. When it came to the point where Terri wanted me to stay at her house, I needed to speak to her daughter. I approached her with respect, because it was her home too. It was not my house. She was not my daughter.

As I was building my relationship with Terri, I also had to build a relationship with her daughter. It was the open communication that Gunn had talked about. I had to gain her trust and earn respect. I knew she trusted her mother, and now she would trust me.

I was a widower, and Terri was a divorcee. We had two different views about being single with children. Her ex-husband was still alive and still had a relationship with his daughter. I had to acknowledge that relationship, accept it, and respect it.

When we did marry, our kids were all adults, spanning ages 19-26, and they had their own lives. I had grandchildren I also brought to the marriage. Her daughter was the maid of honor and my sons were the best men. My oldest grandson, age 6, was ring bearer.

Love and respect have gone a long way in making our blended family work.

I had to respect the relationship of my stepdaughter and her father. Why should I interfere with it? That is their relationship. My relationship with my stepdaughter is our relationship.

My wife also had to respect the fact the boys had a mother. Yet, my wife treated them like they were her own children.

A big benefit to having adult children is that there were no discipline issues. The kids were old enough not to need it.

Blended families face challenges in disciplining, especially when the new parent disciplines the kids. The new parent isn't their biological parent, even though that is the new role they take on. Be open and honest while communicating about roles, responsibilities, parental authority, respect and loving each other and the kids as individuals.

Parents must be on the same page about discipline and trust, and make sure the kids know that you are a parental unit. Blended families can work if you love enough. And isn't love about making relationships, all relationships, work?

Cemetery

How often do I visit the cemetery?

Visiting the cemetery is what I saw old people do. They go to a gravestone. They bring flowers. They pray or say a few words. Why is it we visit a gravestone?

I would visit the site where my father, and then my mother, where buried. I would remember them and our relationship. My mother lived long enough to pick out the gravestone for the both of them.

Picking out a gravestone was not a task I looked forward to at age 39, but it had to be done.

After the stone was cut, after the name and dates were inscribed on it, and it was set in place, it marked the place where the body of my dead wife lay.

Living a plane ride away, I would only get back to town a couple of times a year. I felt compelled to visit the gravesite when I was in town. Whether it was summer or winter, I would visit.

My friends who lived in the area told me they would visit and plant flowers.

When I visited the site, I would look at the front of the stone with my last name on it. I would touch the stone. Feel the rough top and the smooth face of it. I would look at the back and read her name and birth and death dates that were etched in stone. I would trace letters and numbers with my fingers. I would shake my head.

I would shake my head in sadness that she had died. Shake my head in acceptance that the life we had hoped for had ended for her, at this gravesite.

Yet, I knew the only thing here was her body.

Her body is in a casket that was in a container in the ground. The headstone was a marker to locate the body. That was all that was here. But it is the last place she was at.

I am drawn to the last place she was at, just as I was drawn to her in real life. Yet her life is not here at the cemetery. Her life is in the memory of all those who knew her.

The cemetery is the place where we go to visit and remember the dead. Many people cite cemetery etiquette to follow, and ways to visit to make the most of your visit.

Visiting a gravesite often is recommended. It helps the soul feel connected and gives us a chance to talk to our loved ones, albeit a one-sided conversation. But I had many of those after she died. Talking about what is going on is a way to stay and feel connected. I do not know what the spiritual world holds and if these conversations ever get heard on the other side, but we hear them. We hear what we want and that can help us.

"Visiting a cemetery can bring a sense of normalcy and healing to an individual," according to J.P Weiss, a writer and former law enforcement officer. It can also be a time of reflection about our past life and the present. Most research says to visit a cemetery at least once a year because that is a time to pay respects and to reflect.

In the cemetery, we are surrounded by silent reminders of people who had lives. They are now gone, but who remembers them? What type of life did they lead? Standing in a graveyard, we can reflect that we are mortal, as well as reflect on the type of life we are living. Are we being good fathers, mothers, friends, or husbands or wives? And were we good husbands or wives? Is there something we want to change?

When I visited, I would talk to her. A one-sided conversation was taking place, but it reminded me of what we had done, and what she had missed. It is a bittersweet conversation. It confirms that I am living as expected.

Visiting a cemetery brings us in touch with family or friends that used to be in our lives. We pay them respect for having gone before us. We pay respect for having had them in our life. We reflect on where we are now, and how to live, because one day, a family member or friend will stand at our grave. They will remember us. They will be sad that we are gone, but I hope that they will smile that they knew us.

Children

How do I talk to children about death?

Talking to children about death is not that hard: you just leave all your adult words, knowledge, and experiences behind. When talking to kids under the age of 13, you need to fill in the blanks, so they understand.

Kids understand what is going on even if they cannot put it into adult terms. And why should they be expected to use adult terms when they are kids? As adults, we know the adult terms and shortcuts in understanding, and we need to translate those terms into kids' terms.

"Use clear words and honesty to communicate. The news of the death should be said directly even if it seems cold," says Lisa Milbrand writing in Parent's Magazine. Kids do not have the same level of emotions as adults do because they do not understand the concept of death.

I found this to be true when I told my boys about their mother's death. The boys were 6-and-a-half and 5 years old. I told them their mother was 'gone', meaning dead, instead of using the word 'dead'. My five-year-old did not interpret the word 'gone' as 'dead'.

He thought she was gone—like she was still in the hospital and gone from home, the way she had been for the past couple of months.

If I had used the term 'died' or 'dead,' he would have understood immediately without any other thoughts. I thought my choice of words was correct, but it did not convey what had happened. I fell into the pattern of wanting to protect my kids from the harsh news of their mother's death. I thought they knew what I meant. My youngest son did not.

If you have kids and are grieving, talk to them, and make them a part of the process. If you do not involve them, they will assume that something is wrong with them. Guide your children through age-appropriate decisions too.

"Because children grieve differently from adults, it's important to keep them involved but also give them space to opt out of some of the funeral activities," says Dr. Jacks.

I did not involve the boys in every funeral decision I made about their mother because of their age, but I had them pick out her headstone. I did not want to be shopping for a headstone at 39 years of age but that was my life.

The boys needed to feel important and be involved because it was their mother. Shopping for a headstone is like shopping for a car; you try to decide on the perfect combination of color and looks. No stone would be right for me because just after her death, I was still having trouble accepting her death. A headstone is a definite and permanent object that indicates that a person is dead. I knew the boys would find a stone that I would like, and I let them look.

I watched the boys search each row of carved stones. They were taking this task very seriously. They were discussing it with each other. A five and a six-year-old, working together. Finally, they called me over to show me a piece of polished black granite. Etched on its surface was a lighthouse on a rocky shore. The waves are quietly crashing on the rocks.

We talked. I questioned them as to why they had picked this one. They felt the lighthouse was mom—a signal to people she helped. The rocky coast was her disease, and the waves were working to defeat it. They both wanted it. I agreed with them that the stone represented mom's life. I bought it.

We had a private viewing of my late wife's body for the family. I told the kids that the body would look like mom, but it was not her. At the viewing, my five-year-old reached out and touched his mom's arm. I think he was making sure it was real or trying to gauge whether it was or was not her. I did not bring the kids to the cemetery for the burial. I had friends watch them. I felt that that would have been too much. It was too much for me.

"By talking to kids in an open, honest, and age-appropriate way, you can help them understand and cope," says Deborah Serani, Doctor of Psychology writing in Psychology Today.

I talked to them and told them that I would like to get married again someday. They asked what would happen if the new mom did not like them—a good and reasonable question. They wanted to know what would happen to them, and if I loved them and would leave them just like mom did.

I told them, and not just once but many times, that the three of us were a team. If a woman didn't like them, then I wouldn't marry her. I meant it too. We were a team. Someone takes all of us or none of us. I would not give up on my kids just to satisfy myself. I felt that that was especially important for them to know.

On their mom's birthday, we talked about how to celebrate it. We celebrated her birthday with a cake for many years until celebrating her birthday did not seem important.

On the kids' birthdays, I would tell them about the day they were born and what their mother and I were doing that day before their birth, like remodeling the house, and how we felt and about having children.

I let my children grieve in their own way which Dr. Serani encourages. Which was grieving, then playing. Sometimes they were angry and acted out, which was normal. But I let them grieve in their own way and accepted that they would grieve differently than me.

Most of all, we were a team. We went to the movies together. We traveled and vacationed together. We did school trips together. They did not go on dates with me. That would have been inappropriate.

When your children are grieving, be open and direct when talking about death and grieving. Let them know it is okay to grieve and express that grief with words, emotions, and tears. Let them know you are grieving as well and may cry or be depressed too. Give them your time and reassurance that you will be there for them. Tell them that you are not leaving. Let them know that you and they will be okay.

Coping

How do I cope after the death of a loved one?

How you cope with daily living after a loved one dies is important and challenging at the same time. It is hard to wake up in the morning and going to sleep at night is to be feared. There are activities that can help us go through the motions. Through my experience, I found tried and true approaches and tips to reduce suffering and bring the surviving person back into life.

When all was said and done, I gained help from several sources and activities. Here are my top seven tips to return to health and happiness after losing a loved one:

Journal your feelings without holding back—allow yourself to vent every thought, feeling and emotion, regardless of how "good or bad" they seem to you.

Enlist support and help from your local hospice or bereavement group.

Give yourself permission to take "as long as it takes" to recover.

When able, do something for someone else. Volunteer to help others.

Take care of yourself by doing things that make you feel better; get regular massages, take long walks, listen to music, or sleep late.

Do something different at holiday time; find new ways to celebrate, establish new traditions.

Talk about your loved one to friends and family; encourage them to say your loved one's name and share their favorite memories with you.

Journaling gave me a safe place to express the un-expressible, and to vent my feelings. Without this outlet, the toll on my health would have been catastrophic. I used journaling to regain my emotional and mental health. Little by little, my own written words charted my healing process.

I took advantage of bereavement counseling offered by our local hospice, Avow, in Naples, Florida. Both my boys and I were helped by the hospice. There I found a support system to bolster my shattered emotions, help me to identify my emotions, guidance to assist in my decision making and programs to help my suffering sons.

Grieving and healing take time. I spent a long time doing both. That is just how my brain and circumstances worked. The time you take is your time. Take the time you need and do not be pressured by others who think they know what the right amount of time is.

Consider volunteering at any organization that you feel passionate about—like literacy, drowning prevention, wildlife preservation, gardening, or anything else that you are interested in. I found that volunteering, especially in my second year of recovery, helped me get outside myself. I started volunteering in my community with Kiwanis International. I joined a local Kiwanis club that helped feed the hungry, paint houses, repair poor people's homes, helped Habitat for Humanity, and other local nonprofits helping our community. My kids even help during certain activities.

The physical labor felt good and it made other people smile. I keep volunteering which helps me create a community of caring friends and feel useful.

Taking care of my body was helpful too. A friend dragged me to the gym three days a week to workout. The gym, walks, and bike riding helped me keep in good physical condition and gave me time to think. It strengthened my physical being, which added to my health and self-image, and reduced stress.

At the holidays, I tried to make it great for my kids. Even though I did not care to be jolly, I wanted to build good memories for the kids. I still visited with friends, and their holiday spirits helped cheer me up.

Talk about your loved ones if you feel up to it. You and your deceased loved one had a life with friends, parties, and other good times. Take the lead and talk about it. There will be happiness and laughs—yes, laughs—as you recount some stories.

Because I took steps to help myself through these darkest of times, I was able to cope with the stress of living day-to-day without my wife. I started doing small things for myself and for others. As I healed, I did more to get out of my grief.

Even though I did not think I could cope or be happy, the steps I took helped me in meaningful ways. Keep a journal, get out of the house, volunteer, take your time, create new holiday routines and new memories. They helped me pull through, reduce my stress, and return to a happy life.

Coping with the death of a loved one is challenging, especially when we are at a loss as to what to do to help ourselves. I encourage anyone suffering from grief to try the seven tips. You never know which one, or a combination of them, will be the key to helping you reduce your stress and heal from your loss.

Counseling

Does grief counseling really work?

I had an expectation of grief counseling based on what I had read about and heard about counseling. I had gone to counseling before, for other life issues, so I had no fear of counseling. I did not know more than that. I found grief counseling emotionally painful, tough, and challenging. I also found that grief counseling helped me in more ways than I had expected—it did so in four distinct ways.

First, it helped me connect with other grieving people, so I knew that I was not alone.

Second, it helped me identify the feelings and emotions I was going through.

Third, by identifying those feelings, I knew I was not crazy, just grieving.

Fourth, I learned from the group.

Connecting is important. When my wife died, I only saw a few of my immediate family members who were also grieving. But I could not relate to them, because it was my wife; I had the kids. My family was in different stages and had different views of grief, and we did not talk about our grief.

In the grief group sessions at the hospice, I was face-to-face with 20 or so people who were grieving like me. I was not alone. There were others, and that was a comfort. I could feel for them because I knew the feelings we all had. I could share with them and they would understand what I was saying. People who have not experienced the loss of a loved one have trouble understanding the range of emotions that come with this loss.

Identifying my feelings helped me. Grief counselling was able to show me that what I was feeling was normal and part of the process. I did not know about grief attacks before the group. I had a hard time identifying my anger and despair, but the group helped me see those feelings, so I could work on them. The group helped me grow and accept what I was going through.

I was not crazy after all. In the group, I was able to see that the highs and lows were not signs of craziness. They were the normal pathway of grieving. This was good to know, because there were many times when I felt like I was going crazy.

I could see my growth, acceptance, and adjustment by seeing what others were dealing with, or how they were not dealing with issues. Some people seemed stuck on certain issues and talked about it over and over. I could see that I accepted certain issues that others could not. That does not mean those people were wrong. It just meant that they needed more time on that issue, just like I needed more time on certain issues.

After the first year of counseling, I joined another group whose focus was moving on from grief to life issues. This group assumed we had dealt with the first year's hard grief.

Grief counseling groups and individual counseling helped me recognize what I was going through and offered support during the time I was there. The groups cannot cure or heal grief. That is up to you. They offer an ear to listen to you and help you find your way along the grief path that is littered with potholes of emotions.

"Counseling helps you to adjust," says Emily Long, a Licensed Practical Counselor at GoodTherapy.com, "...to the new reality that you are living, such as lifestyle, location, responsibilities, a new way of life, and new ways of connecting with friends and family."

I related to my friends and family differently because part of me was missing. I had to learn how to talk about my life again because I was not part of a couple anymore. Not only was that an adjustment, but now I was living in a new state, adjusting to the weather, vegetation, roads and drivers, directions, architecture, and neighborhoods and neighbors.

My routine changed because the kids entered elementary school nine months after their mother died. Entering school entailed a whole new culture, routine, responsibilities, and adults to interact with, while I was grieving. The kids also had grief counselling. It gave them the same feelings of connectedness that it gave me.

Yes, grief counseling helped me adjust to a new life by showing me what I was going through. It offered tips on how to handle the emotions and changes that were taking place, and also showed me that overcoming grief is relative.

Grieving is hard work. You must face it each day until it slowly slips away from your day-to-day living. We do not all grieve the same way, at the same time, or for the same amount of time. Yes, counseling helped me, it has helped others, and it can help you too.

Dating

Do I have to date?

To date or not to date, that is the question. Whether you are old or young, there is a desire for a relationship with people. But does that mean dating? It depends on your age and circumstance.

When I was growing up, dating was a challenging activity. It was fun, rewarding, and hurtful too. I never questioned that I wanted to date. I just dated. I wanted a partner, and dating was the way to learn what type of woman I wanted, what type I did not want, and learn how to act as a couple.

A year and half after my wife died, I was 41, and I was in the 'life after grief' group. This group was focused on life issues, assuming we had already dealt with grief. One subject that came up was dating.

Dating? What? Are they kidding me? I had trouble getting out of bed and they wanted to talk about dating?

At 41, I still had a long life ahead of me, and I wanted to remarry someday. The point of talking about dating was getting us used to the idea that we could date if we wanted to. We had to see that possibility. We had to figure out if we wanted to date or not. Just thinking about dating was a big hurdle.

I did hang out with a widow, but I did not consider that dating. That was having a friend who knew what the other was going through. It was a support group of two.

I had one date in the first year and all we did was stare at each other. I had nothing to talk about but grief and death, and who wants to talk about that? It is ironic that I was in counseling to talk about grief, but I could not talk about grief on a first date. How could I date, or talk, or even act like I was interested in a woman again when I was still grieving? I didn't feel I was ready to date.

When I thought about dating, I thought about finding a woman just like Lisa—one who would fit in with the life the boys and I were living. We would not have to change at all. She would just drop in and fill that void. Yet, as sociologist Dr. Pepper Schwartz said in an AARP article on sex and love, "...it's unlikely you'll ever meet an exact replica of the one you were with. And let us face it—would you really want to? After all, the person you met at age 25 changes over a lifetime, and so do we. Now as widows and widowers, we are in a different stage and age of life."

I was in a different stage, and I was a different person too. Grief does that to you. Dating when I was single, and now at forty with two kids, felt the same: I felt awkward, didn't know what to say, and was looking for way too much too fast. I had to start somewhere, but first things first. Guilt. Dr. Schwartz also said, "Banish the notion that you are somehow 'betraying' him or her by seeing someone new."

That is easier said than done.

Being newly single, I did not know how to make small talk or conversations that didn't involve death and dying. I had my life uprooted and scrambled, and dating was giving me a chance to get input on how I was adjusting to my new life.

I wanted to date because I wanted to find happiness again—this involved finding comfort, companionship, relationships, and marriage. Dr. Schwartz also said, "The will to live fully again, *and* even experience companionship, will arise."

I joined different interest groups hoping to meet people.

Part of dating again is getting your friends and family used to the idea that you could be with someone other than their son or daughter, sister or brother, best friend, or neighbor.

In my second year of widowhood, I was invited to a wedding. My sons, only seven and six years-old, were in the wedding party as ring bearers. They looked cute in their tuxedos.

I decided to bring a date to start the process of becoming comfortable with a woman who was not my late wife, and I wanted others to see me with a woman who was not my late wife. I mean, it is going to be strange enough to see myself with another woman, but I also must get other people used to seeing me with another woman too.

At the wedding reception, my date and I sat at a table with the boys, my parents, and father-in-law Carl. This was the first time Carl saw me with someone other than his daughter. It felt strange but it was a necessary step in moving forward. It felt good to have someone to dance with and talk to, even if it felt a little awkward around my parents and Carl.

Dating as a widower is hard work.

It is tiring. I could only talk about the same grief issues. What do I talk about if not what my late wife or my recent widowhood? Dr. Schwartz recommends avoiding over-reminiscing about your old life—it may make your new acquaintance feel excluded. "Try to remember that you are not just a widow or widower; you are a person with opinions, hobbies, preferences, accomplishments, social values, political views, and a unique way of looking at the world.

"As you think about how to present your authentic self, be selective about which of those attributes you share right away, and which are best kept private until you get to know a new person better," advises Dr. Schwartz.

This advice is worth considering. It is part of moving from the couples' perspective to the single's perspective. See the chapter 'We to Me' for more on that perspective.

As I dated, I wondered if I was simply scared of finding the right one. Because if I found the right one, that would mean forgetting Lisa, or so I thought. There is no forgetting the past love but there is moving from the hurt emotions to happier emotions. Even at 60 years of age, I can remember parts of me when I was 5 years old. The past is always a memory or an emotional thought away.

I know what I had with Lisa, and I was looking for that again. Maybe I was looking too hard? Maybe I was being too picky? I met many women, yet I got tired of dating and tired of not finding what I was looking for. Sometimes I would go out by myself because it was easier. Sometimes I did not plan well and wound up alone on the weekends.

Over my years of dating, I have met and dated many nice women. We enjoyed our times together, laughed, went out in public, and enjoyed life. Yet each relation only lasted a short time.

I was giving a talk on my grief journey at the Hospice of the Valley in San Jose, California.

After the talk, two women came forward and said I was their hero.

Why, I asked.

They said I was their hero because I didn't get married right away.

It is interesting that they saw men getting married quickly after losing their spouses. Where did it leave these widows? Still alone and looking for a good man? Why couldn't the men wait? There are people who need other people around and cannot stay single.

One aspect of dating was the physical relationship. How soon was too soon to enter a physical relationship? That is up to the people themselves to decide. I had physical relationships too but there were issues there as well—the biggest one was that I had kids.

I rarely took a woman home to meet the kids. I did not feel it was right for them to get their hopes up or for them to get attached to a woman if I wasn't sure. I also did not bring women home for the night.

I thought it would be a bad example and be disrespectful to my kids. What would it be like for them to wake up and see a strange woman in their house? And it was their house too. I wanted them to have the example that sleeping together, and sex, were for marriage, not just a casual affair. I had casual affairs but not in front of the kids.

After several years, I noticed a pattern and I knew I was in a dating rut. The rut was 6 months of dating and 6 months of emotional recovery from dating. Like I said, I met and dated many women who were genuinely nice, attractive, and engaging, but I always found some reason or excuse for them to end the relationship. I was guilty of cowardice. I let them end it when I should have. This type of behavior was cited by Lisa Fritscher in her article Fear of Intimacy, where she said serial dating can be a sign of fear of intimacy.

Also, one woman pointed out that I was clinging to the 'pity me' routine. I was angry at that because I didn't think I was using pity. That was not what I wanted. But when I analyzed my behavior, that is what I was doing, and I had to accept that I needed to change my mindset. So, I decided to change the way I was dating. A few months later, I met Becky.

We were introduced by family members. We dated a year and a half. I ended the relationship. I could not see any future with her. Yet, a month after I last saw her, I looked at pictures of her and smiled. I longed to see her, but I did not follow through. Three days later, I received news that she had been killed in a motorcycle crash.

It was too late for me to do anything but grieve, be depressed, feel guilty and angry.

Not wanting to lose another good woman, I started dating Ann. This seemed like an easy relationship, but it had its moments, and we even became engaged. A month after being engaged, things fell apart in this rebound relationship. Ann pushed all my emotional buttons: loss, respect, rejection, and trust. I was sad at the loss but did not encounter the emotions that Lisa or Becky's death had brought up. It was just sad.

What was I to do?

I was a widowered at 39, and now I was 55. Dr. Schwartz recommends taking stock and then retool for the next phase of life. My reaction to Ann was to go back to school for a Master's in Business Administration (MBA) because that is what I needed at that time and I didn't want to date anymore.

I was done with dating. By going to school, I was hiding from life, escaping grief, in a constructive way.

Going for my MBA took up all my free time. Just like I had thought. I was on a four-year track to get my MBA. There were 3 semesters each year, and I took a class each semester, with a 3-week break in between. On those breaks, I would get on my motorcycle and ride for a week or two to clear my mind. I would clock over a thousand miles on those rides.

A year and a half into my MBA, near the end of the fall semester, I was at my weekly Kiwanis meeting when a woman walked into our club. She was a guest. She was about my height, spikey gray and black hair, black glasses, with a surgical walking boot on her left foot from bunion surgery, and a smile on her face. I was the first person who greeted her. Her name was Terri, and I directed her to the person she was seeking.

For the next two months at the weekly meetings, we would chat. She was divorced. But I noticed that I started to act differently around her. At the meetings, I kept looking for where she was sitting. Then I made sure I was seated at her table. I would say things in front of her that were meant for her ears only. What was I doing? I couldn't understand it. Then I realized I was attracted to her.

As Dr. Carmen Harra, a best-selling author, psychologist, and relationship expert said, an 'Ah ha' moment is when you know this was the relationship you had been working towards.

Realizing this, I asked her out.

I was on school break in January and we went out for dinner. We got to know each other and agreed to go out again. Then school started and I plunged into schoolwork. It was a month later when I asked her out again. Too late—she was dating someone else. Oh well, I thought, I still saw her at Kiwanis meetings and talked with her. Her summer plans and mine would bring us both to New England.

I shipped my motorcycle to Massachusetts, and at the end of the semester, flew up to meet it. Terri was in Rhode Island and we agreed to meet. I rode down. I met her family. She and I went out for dinner and talked. We decided to keep seeing each other. I rode my motorcycle back to Florida.

She knew I was in school and was willing to work around the time that I had free and date me. I wanted school to be over so I could spend more time with her.

A year later we went on a vacation by motorcycle. It was our one-year dating anniversary. We talked about all the things that had happened in the past year and what the future held. It was then that I pulled out the engagement ring and proposed to her. She accepted.

Four months later, I received my MBA. Another three months later—7 months from our engagement—we were married in front of friends and family. We now have a blended family.

Over my 20 years of widowhood, I dated many women. Each woman was unique, but I could not see the long-term in many of them. Some were casual dates, other hinged on the serious. My decisions in each case were made by my gut feeling. But I dated to help me find the right woman for me. Some people find someone in a shorter time. I just took longer.

It doesn't matter how long it takes to find the right person. We each have our own issues, our loss, and our families to consider. When it is right, you will know it. Even though that phrase sounds corny or unbelievable, which it did to me too, I did know when it was right.

Whether you date again or not is up to you. I know older widows who didn't date because they felt they had already had the best there was. Younger people may date or not. Some marry within a year or wait. Dating, just like grieving, has its own timetable. You will know when it is right.

Death and dying

What are the universal realities of death and dying?

Religion and politics are two subjects regarded as most abhorred in polite company, but there is one that is even more verboten: talk related to death and dying.

Why is it difficult to talk about the end of our life or the lives of our friends and loved ones? Why do we avoid the topic of death at all cost? Death is as much a part of life as birth. The more we talk about it and explore various beliefs, the more we demystify it and remove the "too terrible to talk about" voodoo curse of it. Then we are free to relax and accept it.

How peculiar is it that since not one of us is getting out of here alive?

But the truth is—our mortality terrifies us.

Granted, there is a community that deals with death and dying, which includes lawyers, doctors, nurses, funeral homes, counselors, and therapists. They work crafting wills and trusts. They prepare bodies for funeral viewing. Counselors and therapists help those left behind deal with their emotional trauma. Grief support groups offered by hospices, churches, and mental health associations are widely available. Yet conversations with our friends rarely touch on the subject.

The words we use to describe the person who died sometimes depends upon our closeness to the deceased, the length of time since they died and our willingness to be vulnerable. We use terms to describe what happened such as our loved one is deceased, lost, late, has passed on, made their transition, is dead, died, or departed. The deceased often leaves behind a spouse, or significant other, children, sisters, brothers, cousins, friends and sometimes parents, and even grandparents. Often the departed leave behind in their wake a void that is huge—the number of people profoundly impacted by that death is great.

One death is like a pebble dropped in a still lake. The closer you are to the center the more the hurt, but the waves ripple outward to the family and friends, community members, neighbors, business associates, church congregants and their families.

Over 6,700 people die each day in the United States. Factor in their family members, friends, and business colleagues to see the exponential impact each death has. It is not unusual for thousands of people to be touched by one death—yet so few people want to talk about death and dying.

Why is it difficult talking about the end of our lives? Why is it difficult to talk to an attorney about what to do with our accumulated stuff after we die? Why does making out a living will prior to surgery make us gulp? Don't we need to be prepared?

Perhaps we fear death because we have no control over how or when we die. Thinking of ourselves as not being alive on earth is unimaginable. Just as birth brings us into the world of light and air, death takes us away. Where we were before and where we go after death sparks much debate. The answers depend on personal and religious beliefs.

Widows, widowers, and parents who have lost a child, know all too well the disbelief, guilt, depression, and despair that often overwhelms those left behind. Grief can be ignored for a while, but it doesn't go away until we face it, deal with it, and accept it. We must go through that process to know laughter, joy, happiness, and the bitter-sweet satisfaction of living again.

"Nothing is more shocking, emotional, or final than the death of a loved one," says Dr. Paul David Tripp, pastor, event speaker, and a best-selling and award-winning author. In fact, it makes no sense at all.

Recognizing your deep feelings and allowing the grief to be expressed will make all the difference. Share with a trusted friend and keep a journal of your thoughts and feelings. Grab onto a lifeline, seek professional help from a therapist or counselor who is a 'death and dying' expert. Often hospices offer qualified, thoughtful, loving, and exceedingly helpful professionals with whom you can meet in a one-on-one or group setting.

Being able to talk and write about what you are going through and how you feel will make all the difference in the world. Expressing your pain, your regrets and your aching loss, is the path to healing without question. Yes, it seems impossible that you will ever smile again, enjoy life, or wake up with a light heart. The sooner you give grief its due, the sooner you will have a life worth living again.

Shakespeare knew the route to healing grief:

"Give sorrow words. The grief that does not speak whispers the o'erfraught heart, and bids it break." —*Macbeth*

Yes, we will all die one day. Whether it is from disease, an accident, or just old age, we will all die. Being prepared for that event is wise. Why leave our loved ones, not only guilt-ridden and depressed, but with all our stuff to save or discard. We can help them by acknowledging our mortality and leaving behind memories and not just items to agonize about.

We can talk to those we love about what we want for our funeral, and the stuff we have accumulated.

We can help the living by accepting our mortality and planning for a good death.

Doing it all

What to do when your spouse did it all?

I was a month shy of my 40th birthday when I walked into my first hospice group. The other widows and widowers were, for the most part, 70 or 80 years old. There were few people close to my age. We all had our roles in our marriage: whether housekeeper or breadwinner. As widows or widowers, we must learn what our spouses did for us in our marriage.

What did our spouses do for us? There are women learning how to do home repairs or how to call repairmen or pay bills. Men are learning how to handle the checkbook or cooking. There is something new that each person must learn.

I had been the at-home parent and did the cooking and raising of our kids. Lisa, my wife, was the breadwinner with the responsibility of making the big decisions on doctors, and other things and people that we needed. After her death, I was a single parent. I did not have that helping hand—that special someone, who wanted to hear every little story of what the kids did that day. Our boys were only 5 and 6 at the time of Lisa's death.

I had to learn to be the responsible one for the family. I had to find a pediatrician. I had to interact with the school and the other parents. I had to support the kids' sports programs and host their friends. I had to manage the finances and the house.

Finding a pediatrician was a necessity but it was something that I had never done alone. Filling in the forms with my late wife's name was depressing.

At school, they let parents volunteer, which I liked. When I volunteered, I was typically the only dad at the event. I had to be there on Mother's Day, Valentine's Day, Special friends' Day, and for plays and sporting events. I also had to be present on parents' night and listen and ask questions of the teachers when we talked about the kids' classroom behavior and abilities. I had no spouse who could offer advice or ask questions different than me.

Being a single dad with boys was easier when my sons' friends came over to the house, as most of them were boys. I could understand the roughhousing, the immense quantity of food they would eat, and the talk and banter.

When they started sports, I was the 'sports' dad. At little league games, I was in the stands with the other parents or helping in the concession stand. I was the lone male parent among the married couples.

Like all widows or widowers, all the house decisions fell on my shoulders. Whom to call when there was a burst pipe? What improvements did I want to do? Do I handle them myself or call in a professional?

I could paint the interior of the house myself. If I made a mistake or didn't like the color, then I repainted it. I was handy and could replace toilets, doorknobs, and other stuff, if needed.

Picking out furniture came down to my choice. There was no spouse to consult with. I did ask the boys a couple of times, but they really did not care that much. The feminine touch was lost in the house, and our house became a bachelor's pad.

In our grief group, we were all grieving and we had to learn new responsibilities of a role that our late spouses used to do. No matter what that new thing was, we had to learn it. And we had to do this on top of grieving. All this added to the feeling of being overwhelmed. It seemed like we couldn't do it all.

A hospice can offer much in the way of healing from grief. Groups can offer formats where we can discuss our new roles and what we must learn. Learning all the new skills is up to us. It is our life. We can learn to do it ourselves, or whom to call. If we make a mistake, we can try not to repeat it. Check your community resources for opportunities to learn the new skills that you need to know. You will make it through.

Dreams

Why do I dream of the dead?

Dreams can be fun, interesting, confusing, startling or unnerving. Dreams of our past loved one can be any of the above. Can dreams of our past loved ones be signs from the other side? Can they be proved, or do they have to be proved if they are our dreams?

I dreamed of my wife after she passed. It was natural to still want her. The dreams I am talking about are those where the deceased loved one appears in our dreams and sparks the recognition of that person as real. You know who they are.

My late wife visited me in several dreams.

The first time I dreamt of her, I saw her standing in a field. I could see her, the setting, and her hair was flowing. We came together and hugged. I could feel that hug. It was warm and comforting, and it felt just like I was hugging her in real life. She told me she had to go, and I said I know. When I woke up and remembered the dream, I knew that she meant she couldn't stay in the physical world. It was comforting—it gave me peace. I could accept that she was gone, and that she had no choice in the decision.

I still missed her, but I did find comfort in the dream. It seemed real and right.

The second dream was disturbing. I was lying in bed and I had fallen asleep. She was in the room and sat on the bed beside me. I could feel the weight of her sitting on the bed too. I could see the scars across her abdomen from the series of operations she had had. I woke up startled because it seemed so real. I was confronted with her operations in a way I had not done while she was alive. It was disturbing.

My second wife had dreams of her late father. We had just returned to Florida after his funeral service. That night, in her dream, she felt him in the room—it was a presence at the foot of the bed on her side of the bed. It scared her at first, yet she felt he was telling her that he was okay. It happened two nights in a row, then stopped.

Another time she saw him walking down a hill. He was wearing a fedora. He was as skinny as he was in real life. When he was close, he had a blank expression on his face, but he gave her a strong hug like he used to do in real life. She woke up with tears in her eyes because she missed his hugs. The dream was so real.

Are these signs that the deceased loved ones have shown us?

How do we know it is real? According to Blair Robertson, a psychic medium, he says in his blog that when we see our loved ones in a dream, and their features are clear just as their characteristics are, then it is a visitation. A regular dream doesn't have many details.

"That is the difference," said Robertson. "Our loved ones can act like they did in real life, or not. There are no rules."

That is why my wife and I believe that in our dreams we interacted with the deceased. The details were clear, they acted and felt like they did in real life, and they gave us a message that they were okay.

The dreams can be helpful in healing from a loss says Marilyn Mendoza, Ph.D., a clinical instructor in the psychiatry department at Tulane University Medical Center. Dreams tend to vary according to how long the loved one was gone, how they died, and our relation to them. Dreams can reassure us, give us a message of comfort, and be positive.

My wife and I believe they were real because we felt the presence of the person in ways that were unique to us. The dreams, for the most part, were reassuring and positive.

People will say that they are just dreams and have no real connection with the deceased. They can say that. It may be true for them. But I know what I felt and the message that I received. They were real to me, and that matters to me.

Whether you have dreamt of your loved ones or you haven't, that is okay. We grieve differently. Whether you believe in dreams or not is okay. There are people who dream of their deceased loved ones and feel that connection with them. Grieving is hard and different for everyone. If you feel good about dreams, then accept them because that is part of your process of acceptance.

Escaping

Can I escape grief?

Most professional counselors say you must grieve your loss. It can be delayed but at some point, grief must be worked through, accepted, and assimilated into your life.

But can you escape grief?

"No, because you never get over your loss," says Mary Lamia, Ph.D., a clinical psychologist and psychoanalyst. "As time passes, the intensity of feelings about the loss will lessen. You might also find ways to sooth or distract yourself."

Some people escape grief by using alcohol, drugs, pornography, or any other addictive behaviors and substances. Some behaviors can be destructive. Other behaviors can be constructive or inconsequential.

I found two ways to escape grief: one was through child's play, and the other through volunteer work.

After my wife died, I knew that my 6 and 5-year-old sons were going to save me. On a conscious level, I didn't know how they were going to do that. I just knew they would. I still had to process my grief and go through the emotions. As adults, we grieve all the time—grief is at the forefront of our thoughts and emotions, and in our hearts. My life before grief had all the joy and fun—the way children see the world—but my life with grief seemed devoid of the goodness, love, and possibilities.

Children grieve differently than adults. Children grieve, then go play, and then grieve again. To most children, the world is full of cookies and candy, promise and possibilities, and goodness and love. Everything is new and the possibilities are endless.

My kids allowed me to escape from dealing with grief. It is only now, many years down the road from grief, that I realize how they helped me escape: they gave me a temporary avenue to escape my adult world of responsibilities and proper adult behavior. I didn't give up my adult responsibilities. But I was able to, in my mind and for short periods of time, become a child and leave the adult world behind.

How did I do this? By following their lead in the world of play.

One afternoon, a Florida rainstorm was rolling in. I challenged my sons to see who could stand out in the rain the longest. It was a simple, stupid, and yet an effective way of being a child. We leaned against the car and were pelted by the heavy afternoon thunderstorm. After the rain, we jumped in the mud puddles. I was physically getting my grief out without thinking about it. It worked by helping me divert my mind from dwelling on grief.

When I ventured into the kids' world, I was leaving the grieving and the adult responsibilities of the 'I must pay the bills, get dinner ready, prepare the kids for school or repair the house' behind. It was an escape that was an acceptable outlet for me, a bonding moment with my kids, and a healing process for us all. We were all together in the grief journey.

Being a single parent responsible for a family and home is hard enough without the grieving process. Escaping to the kids' world, even for a minute, took me far away from my grieving life. It brought a bit of sanity to my crazy world.

For my kids' birthday party, I did the traditional cake-and-gifts thing in the house. But after that, it was outside for a whipped cream and water balloon fight. The kids loved it. The other parents thought I was crazy and wanted to see it for themselves. There were some minor injuries but no bloodshed. I am sure the kids will remember it for the rest of their lives. I would have loved it as a kid.

My kids may or may not remember those small interactions, but to me, those escape routes where I acted like a child, helped heal my adult brain.

What if you don't have kids or grandkids? How can you escape grief for a time?

Then you need to find a recreation center or a group of people that play board games, sports, or other mind-distracting activities to help you escape from grief, even for a little while.

Through volunteer work and exercise, I was able to leave my grief behind because my focus was on doing something for someone else. I was doing those tasks to the best of my ability, and that meant I had to focus on that project to get it right. I was not grieving at those times.

One time I was delivering Thanksgiving meals to people who were struggling. I had my youngest son with me. We were delivering food to a young woman. She cried with happiness that someone had thought of her. I felt good to be helping, and it made an impression on my son too.

Full-time grief work is exhausting. Give yourself a break and let your mind be free. You can join an activity center and learn something new, play computer games, play a sport, enjoy the kids, or volunteer. The main point is to get your mind focused on a task to escape from grieving for a little while. The grief will wait for you.

Father's Day

How do I celebrate Father's Day?

Father's Day recalls all things paternal—working on the house, working in the yard, fishing, bowling, going to work outside the home, and roughhousing with the boys. Father's Day can be extremely challenging for children who have lost a father. Even if schools don't recognize Father's Day, there is enough news of the day to impact a child, and they can remember it well into their older years.

I know the challenge of responding to Father's Day as a single dad. The day brought new meaning to my two sons. I had to be a mother to advise them on what to buy dad on Father's Day.

If you have young children who have lost their father, then obviously you must celebrate the day in ways far different from other children. As a father, I had an idea how to celebrate Father's Day.

I can recommend the following five approaches to help you and your kids celebrate Father's Day if they don't have a father present in their lives. I hope these tips help you.

Remember the good times. Pictures are great for triggering memories. Bring them out and talk to your kids about the day each picture was taken. Share the life you and your husband or significant other were dreaming about and how you felt about having kids. Keep the talk on an age-appropriate level. There will be days to come when they are older and can understand more. Always reassure them that you and they are a team, and you have no intention of leaving them.

Establish new routines. A new routine can be simple or elaborate. June, the month we celebrate Father's Day, is baseball season, so you can take your kids to a baseball game or toss a baseball around at the local field. Build a scrap book of favorite pictures and sayings. Find your special place for your new routine.

Find a "new dad" for the children to honor. This does not mean getting married. It means finding a dad substitute—a brother, uncle, grandfather, or a special male friend that your young children can send cards to, write messages to, or play with. This helps remove the trauma of being a fatherless child in elementary or middle school.

Encourage your kids to write a letter to their dad. When having kids write such a letter, make sure they know that only they and their dad will know what is in it. You might want to put the letters into an envelope for safekeeping. If the kids are open to it, you can read the previous year's letter before writing a new one. You can save their letters and eventually, when the kids are older and get married, you can return the letters to them.

Eat cake. Go to a movie or rent a movie. Kids do not want to sit and grieve. They do not want to sit, period. Get up and get out of the house. Shoot basketballs, throw a baseball, play miniature golf, or go to a zoo or a museum. Enjoy a new day. Create new memories.

Remind your kids that even if their dad is not physically around, they still have a dad who loves them dearly. If your children are in elementary school, remember, there often is a Father's Day card-making activity at school and conversations about dads. It can be a hard time for them. Discuss the day with them ahead of time.

Being a parent is difficult and challenging. Being a single mom with young kids is hard. Help your kids make it through Father's Day by trying new approaches to a tough situation. Both my sons and I not only survived but thrived. I assure you that you and your children can do it too.

Firsts

What are the first 365?

The first year after losing a spouse is the hardest. It is filled with stress, grief, uncertainty, and a roller-coaster of emotions. It is also a year of 'first times' for you.

One reason the first year of losing your loved one is the hardest is that there are 365 'first time' events that will happen to you without your loved one. It is not just the big days like birthdays and anniversaries, but each regular day will be a first, in the first year.

As an example, the first Tuesday you are without your spouse is the first Tuesday. Wednesday is the first Wednesday. The next Tuesday is the second Tuesday but it is also the first second Tuesday of the month. You have survived the first Tuesday. You know you will survive the many firsts that are to come.

Each day of the week for the first year is the first time you have lived that day without your loved one. There are 365 days in that first year. Each day can bring a personal memory of something you did on that day.

Then come the once-a-year events such as holidays, birthdays, and anniversaries. Each one of these special days is a reminder of your loss. The days leading up to the special days, at least for me, were worse than the day itself. I was fearful of losing control or breaking down. I never did on those days, but the fear was there.

More firsts include the first time you go shopping. If you were already the one who shopped, how was this one different? There was no one else to think about when buying food. And single meal prep can be a lonely experience. If shopping for clothes, your loved one isn't there to give you their opinion. How did that make you feel?

If you are taking on responsibilities of your late spouse, then every time you call a repairman, write a check, or redecorate in that first year, will the first time you have done so without your spouse.

I had my first birthday without my wife. The first 4th of July party without her. The kids' first day of school. First summer, winter vacation, and Halloween without her. Even the first time I remembered our engagement without her or thought of our first home together. Thoughts can also be firsts too.

Each day is a new day for each of us because it is the first time we are experiencing that day of that first year without our loved one being alive. They are the first 365 days we experience in widowhood. They are 'first times' because our loved one isn't here for that day.

Three hundred sixty-five days is a long time when grieving. But it is only a year compared to what we have already lived. Time flies as we get older and a year goes by in just the blink of an eye. The first year after losing a spouse or someone dear will be 365 first times of everything. They will involve major events and small events. It is the first year of your new life. It will be Okay.

Forgetting

What is stuck between remembering and forgetting?

There came a time in my grief recovery where I was faced with the acceptance that grieving was done, and now, I had to get on with life. There was the feeling and gnawing in my brain that I had to forget my dead wife to move on, but I wanted to remember her too.

Can I move on and remember and forget her too?

I remember being in kindergarten, a fight in middle school, being embarrassed in high school, and fights with my late wife. Those are parts of my life that I remember but I have moved on from them.

Now here, after grieving or while still grieving the death of my wife, I have memories of her. If I were to move on and not talk about her, is that forgetting her? How can I forget her if I can still remember kids from my kindergarten days? Or the girls I dated in high school?

I cannot forget my late wife.

She was a large part of my life, not just in terms of the number of years that we were married. She had a large emotional impact on my life. We lived and loved together. Had children together. I watched her die. How can I forget all that?

How can you ever forget your loved one?

We can't forget them, but we can move on without being stuck trying to forget and remember them at the same time. What I had to accept is that moving on to my new life did not mean I had to forget my old life or my wife. Moving on is an adjustment.

"Moving on is more about learning to live what I call a 'both/and' life rather than an 'either/or' life. It's not about grieving or forgetting, happy or sad , black or white. It's shades of gray," said Emily Long, a LPC on the Good Therapy website.

It is a mixture of our life. I can still grieve if I must. I can live. I can love. I can walk or drive a car or ride a bike. As Long said, it isn't an 'either/or' situation. We can feel grief and still date. We can be happy and still grieve. We can remember and still create new memories (See How to Create new and Happy Memories.)

I looked at it as an 'either/or' situation but, I was happy to accept that it wasn't. It was both. It is finding that spot where you are okay with your life and accept that you have a loss. The deceased person is a memory, and they will always be in your memory.

The forgetting part is what happens on a day-to-day basis. I know I get dressed every day, but I don't remember what I wore each day. I forget the past daily interactions because I am living now, and those past actions are being replaced with today's actions and interactions. I am building a new life with new memories.

I remember who my late wife was, the love we felt, the fears and the tears. I remember the day I met her, the day we became engaged, the day she died, and other days in between. Pictures help me to remember. But the daily activities of when we held hands, what day did we grocery shop, when did she tell me something her friend did. Those small details are forgotten. The bigger events are remembered.

My day-to-day living creates memories that I may or may not remember in the future. I will remember if I write them down and take pictures of them, but I am not going to record what I wore every day. I have a general idea, if it relates to work or play.

I remember my past married life. I remember the feelings, the love, the joy, and heartbreak. Those are memories we will always have. Just like the memories we have of being six or twelve.

You will forget the day-to-day routines too because they are the common things you do. You will not forget your loved one. You have too many emotional memories of them. You can remember them and build new memories in your life. It is both. Living requires that we live in the present—the past is always a memory. Your late spouse is always in your memory and just a thought away.

Friends

What about our friends?

Friends come from our life before marriage, some we make during marriage, and some after marriage. Friends can be from high school, collage, work, or from our spouses. Friends can be brought into a marriage too. We want our friends to like our spouse and hope they become our friends too.

Before we were married, I had my friends and Lisa had her friends. As we dated, I met some of her friends and they became my friends. She met some of my friends and they became her friends too. As a couple, we also had couples who were our friends.

My friends and her friends came together when we married. They came to our house and we went to their houses. We had parties. We went on vacations together. Those with kids who lived near us came by so our kids could play together. We were comfortable with friends from her side, my side, and the new friends we made as a couple. Our friends even made friends, or became close acquaintances, with each other.

When Lisa passed, the support of our friends helped me make it through the tough beginning of my new life. Life changed as I moved to a new city. All the friends we had were now a thousand miles away. A few friends and coworkers moved to the new city too. That was a big help in adjusting. Now, in a new city, I had to make new friends and grieve at the same time.

But what about the other friends that were first hers, mine, and then ours?

According to Catherine Tidd, widow, writer, and speaker, "...there is a certain training process we have to put our friends through when we lose our significant other. We must show them who we are now. We must give them time to digest who we're becoming."

In the section on dating, I talked about bringing a date to a wedding to show people I could be with someone else and to give me time to adjust to being with someone else too. This is part of the training that Tidd is speaking about: getting friends used to the new you, getting them used to the new single person that you are, and as a person who is dating, instead of part of a couple that they once knew.

I was the one who moved, and I was the one who lost a spouse. I was the one who had to keep up the friendship for as long as possible. Yet, I could not do it all. I could not keep up with everyone who were 'her' friends first, then 'our' friends. Our friends were good to me when I needed them, mostly in the early years of widowhood. For that fact, I am profoundly grateful.

As the years passed, friendships did change. I still had friends that were my friends before my wife passed. I still had friends that were her friends. I still had friends that had been friends to both of us. In my new life, I made new friends as well.

Yet, as I lived so far away, and as the years passed with less contact on my part, people drifted away. "If you want people to be with you," Tidd says, "*You have to call.* Even though you are grieving." Tidd suggests calling your friends because your friends don't know how to act around you either. You have to show them that you are still around. Be open and caring like before. Show them you are not a threat who will take away their spouse. Yes, some people believe that now that you are single, you are a threat to their spouse. They feel threatened that you will cross boundaries and cheat with their spouse. That is a feeling I never had from my friends, or if they felt that way, they didn't tell me. But I have heard it from other people. I cannot imagine crossing those boundaries with my friends. It is not how I view my friends.

Yes, some friends will drift away from you for a variety of reasons: no common interest, you are no longer a couple, threat of stealing their spouse, and the reality of death and grieving, or they miss their friend too much to see you alone or with someone else. Accept that some will leave, and others will stay. If you value the friendships, then step out of grief and make the calls. Stay in touch and show them that you are still a friend and not a threat to their marriage.

Yes, it is extra work you may not feel like doing, especially when grieving, yet the benefits of staying in touch will outweigh the isolation and grief you may be experiencing. Friendships will be stronger, last longer, and will be deeper than ever.

In our second marriage, we brought all our friends with us. Together, as a new couple, we are making friends with other couples too. We still have old friends from our single days, and some from our married days. Other friends have drifted away because I was widowered.

It is okay to reach out to old friends, even years later just to catch up. It may or may not start the friendship up again, but it shows you still think about them and what you had.

Nurture your friends and let them grow with you. If they go by the wayside, accept that they have lives too, and they may not be able to keep in touch. You can also reach out too. We all need friends, and some of the old friends are the best.

Giving in or up

What is giving up or giving in?

Do you think that moving on in life after grief is giving in to the loss or giving up on your deceased spouse? Or is it giving up on recovery and giving in to grief? Why can't 'giving up' and 'giving in' be moving on?

When my wife died, a new chapter of my life began—the life of being a single person after having been married. It is not what I wanted. Most people don't want it, but it happens.

Through grief work, widows and widowers are growing and moving from a couple's perspective to a single's perspective. That process involves resolving the emotions, love, and attachment we had with our deceased loved one. It involves living without that person, and potentially finding someone new. Some of these emotions and thoughts feel disrespectful to our lost partner—like we need to forget them to go forward.

We aren't trying to forget them. We don't want to forget them, but we do need to move on. This struggle goes on as we accept being widowered, and accept that we have a new life, and that people are going to look at us differently. We don't forget, but we have to accept that they are gone.

The person we loved is now a memory—a part of our past, a part of us forever. Thinking of them as a memory is not disrespectful; it is our new reality. We must accept this new reality to heal. They died, and we are living a new reality without them. Just like high school is a memory of our life.

Yes, it hurts. Yes, I wish it wasn't true. It made me feel guilty about living. But it is the continuation of our lives. Accepting our new reality is *giving in* to our new reality, and that feels like we are *giving up* on our past loved one. We aren't forgetting our loved ones. We can't forget them, but we are living without them.

Moving on means giving up the day-to-day routines that we had with our loved one. It means creating new day-to-day routines. And this too will change as we live and learn to adapt to the new single, widowered life. There are so many changes to accept.

We never give up on our loved one. They were a part of our lives that we do not want to forget. There are still people in our lives who we love and who are with us. But the closest one, our spouse, is not. We all know this to be the terrible truth.

We survived the trauma of our loss, and we are on our own. We must give up the couples' life and accept our new single life. The single life is anything you make it. We are accepting and giving in to living without our loved one. We are moving on. We are accepting the natural grieving process by giving in to it. By giving up our old lives, we are accepting our new life.

It is not easy. At first, it involves mental gymnastics, and we perform them to be ourselves without our partner. It involves accepting who we are, and where in the grieving process we are, and trying to cope and live.

By accepting the death of our loved one, we give up the life we used to live. We give in to the reality of the life we are now living. It is accepting that our life has changed, which it has. This move is part of healing and moving away from the fear of loss and adapting to our new life.

Yes, losing our loved one hurts. Yes, I wish it were not true. But we are alive and must give in to the fact that we are widowed. We must give up the old ways of relating to people and accept that we are different. We must accept our new life by giving up our old life and giving in to the new reality.

Going home

What is going home?

There are certain words or phrases, bits of music, or sights that bring me to tears. It is not only for their beauty but for their ability to bring forth the feelings of love and loss that still reside in me. There is grief that lingers on in the memories and emotions associated with our loved ones. One such thought for me is what I call 'going home'.

What is 'going home'?

The thoughts of 'going home' are words that bring me grief. Not quite a grief attack, but to a point where I search for an answer to find out where home is, how to go there, and I wonder exactly what it means.

I moved to a new community about 1,500 miles from where I lived with my late wife. It was going to be 'our' new community. Fifteen hundred miles from where I met my wife, where our kids were born, where our home was, and where she passed.

Home has many meaning and emotions for me, and they were very confusing meanings too because of the old home and the new home. There were more community ties in the old city than in the new. As I lived in the new city, I formed more ties with the community.

I get tired of sadness. I do not grieve all the time or even every day. I would not be able to write this if I grieved all the time! But there are instances when the grief and loss come back, and I think, "Didn't I already deal with that?" I have dealt with it, and I need to deal with it again. It is not the grief of losing my wife but the issues that still linger about things that I can't quite classify. It came after two other losses that I had.

I felt tired of the new community because I associated it with loss. After the two additional losses, I wanted to move. But where, I thought.

I felt like I wanted to go home. But did I think about moving back to the town or state where I grew up? Did I want to move fifteen hundred miles back to where Lisa and I lived as man and wife? I have sold the house so there is no going back there. But something lingered. So, when I think I want to go home, I do not know if I want to go back to where I lived, or long for a part of my past life.

When I see pictures of Boston, and that region of the country, where I spent the first forty years of my life, I get homesick and want to return. It is where my memories of joy, love, friendships and happiness took place. It is the place where I matured physically and emotionally.

Living in Florida began with grieving, pain, loss, and depression. Yet, I have lived in Florida for over 20 years now. A third of my life in a state where I have no roots. A place where I have limited family. It took me years before I could say Florida was my home.

Florida is not worse than any other place. It is simply different. There's a different smell to the air, a different feel to the soil, and a different color green to the vegetation. It is foreign and familiar. The seasons are different. The direction of the coast is different. Instead of heading east to the ocean, I head west to the Gulf of Mexico.

If I stay long in New England, I long for the comforts of my Florida home: my computer, work, taking out the trash, the familiar walls of the home building, and those mundane things.

Because I have kids, now grown, I had a more community-oriented life in Florida with other families than I did up north. I have roots in my community, yet that feeling of home still swirls around the recesses of my brain. What is the resolution?

I have discovered that answer. That answer came to me after I remarried. The answer is with my new wife and our relationship.

When I thought I wanted to go home, I wanted to go to the happy place of love and life. I wanted to go home to the comfort of my wife, the love of my wife, the ability to love, and the happiness and security that was my wife, my partner, and the woman who understands my sense of humor. All of that is what home is for me. That is what I lost when I lost Lisa.

When I want to go home, I want the comfort, the trust, the laughter, and the knowing looks we had that spoke of love and that I can love. Love is home.

My remarriage has given me a new feeling, and now my thoughts of going home have changed. Going home means going home to my wife and the physical and emotional comfort that she brings to my life. I still have friends up north. All those familiar places are still there. I am going home to the comfort of a life where love is given and returned.

It is a cliché that home is where the heart is, but I have found that to be true. Home is where my heart belongs to a new love. I am glad I found my wife and my answer.

I am going home.

If you desire to go home, think about what home means to you. Is it a physical location? Family? Friends? As we grow older, many of our friends move to be near family for the comfort, security, and memories that families make together. As widows and widowers, going home is going to where your heart finds comfort with family, friends, and love. I wish you a good journey.

Grief attacks

What is a grief attack?

What bus just hit me I thought as I broke down and cried. Where did this rush of painful emotions come from? Why did it happen? What is it called? Am I going crazy?

"Just when the bereaved thinks he has made great strides in the healing process, wham! A grief attack strikes," says Dr. Diana Jacks in her book, *Here to There, Grief to Peace*. Dr. Jacks calls this aspect of grief being "blindsided."

Getting blindsided by grief was all too familiar to me. The worst part was I did not know what it was called or if it was normal.

Yes, I was blindsided by grief, and I learned that it would not be the last time.

In hospice counseling, I learned that being rapidly overwhelmed by grief is called a 'grief attack'. The hospice said it is like going crazy. It was like that for me. One moment I thought I was doing fine, and the next moment I stepped off the curb and was hit by the proverbial bus.

Grief attacks come in many forms. Sometimes I cried. At other times, the tears flowed silently.

One night, I was sitting with friends watching television when Mariah Carey came on and sang *Hero*. My friend's daughter had written out the words to the song for me because Lisa, my late wife, was a hero to her. The song came on and the tears started running down my face. There was no sobbing or sounds, just the tears. For me, this was a mild grief attack.

Other grief attacks racked my body with sobbing so hard that I could not continue with what I was doing, never mind think about something positive. Grief attacks are the worst feeling possible.

In the first year after her death, I could not listen to songs on the radio because they made me cry. Talk radio was uninteresting. An advertisement sign could make me cry. A thought could make me cry. It seemed like almost anything that reminded me of Lisa and our love would make me cry.

I know that I cried for what I lost. I also cried for what could have been. It did not matter where I was or who was around when the grief attack came. I just had to roll with it. I let the tears come and wash the grief from my soul so that I could continue with life. I wished that the grief attacks only happened at home because I did not want people seeing me cry. But that was not always possible.

"I'm thinking about the little reminders that in an instant put you into a deep grieving space," said Pat Schwiebert, R.N., writing about grief triggers on the website Grief Watch. She adds, "Where you are distracted from what you were doing and suddenly find yourself in that abyss where nothing else matters but your pain." Sights, sounds and smells are high on the trigger list of items sparking grief attacks, said Schwiebert.

The smell that did it for me was my wife's perfume: Chanel No. 5. It was what she wore and what I would smell when I held her close.

It was a reassuring scent that could connect me, like a trigger, to my past life. At first, it caused grief attacks. As time went on, it was more of a sedative to calm me, bring me good memories and help me remember the joy and love of the past. Eventually, I did not need it to remind me of her.

Ordinary items cause grief attacks—like ordinary pieces of paper, nail files, and tubes of lipstick. Just the ordinary items she used that were part of her.

The road of grief is full of potholes. The potholes are grief attacks. In the beginning of the journey, there are many holes that you can and will fall in. But the further you move away from the traumatic event, the less frequent the holes appear, and they get further and further apart until the road is 99% solid. The 1%? A trigger will get you there, but you will know what it is and go with it. It will not last that long either.

When you start your journey, grief attacks will come sharp and quick. As you travel on, grief attacks will subside as you integrate your past and present life. Grief attacks happen less and less as you move past the hurt and into accepting the loss and the normal flow of life. When a grief attack happens, it will be brief. It will not feel like being hit by a bus anymore. And you will be okay with it because you know what they are.

Grieving

Do I have the strength to grieve?

Crying shows weakness. Showing feelings shows weakness. The idea that grieving shows weakness is a false idea. I believe it takes strength to run headlong into the jaws of grief. Who wants to tangle with emotional pain? Who wants to accept that we are not who we once were? Who wants to accept that our partner in life died?

It takes strength to accept that we are weak. It takes strength to accept that we failed in keeping our loved one alive. Can we accept that we are just human, and we hurt, and we need other people? Can we accept our own mortality and that of our loved ones?

I had all these thoughts and more as I moved through the depression, anger, and acceptance of losing my wife. How could I hurt so much?

As a man, I questioned the basic image and role of a man. Aren't we supposed to save the heroine? All the books and movies have the hero saving the heroine, and I believed that I could do that too, but I could not save my wife from cancer.

Aren't we supposed to be able to stay together till death do us part? My parents did. My wife's parents did. I did. But I know other families that did not stay together till one died. How do I deal with the toughest time in my life without the person who is supposed to be there to support me in the toughest times of my life? I grieved and learned what grief was and woke up every morning to its pain and trudged through it. There was no Option B to this part of my life.

Roberta, my second mother-in-law, was facing similar questions after 55 years of marriage. She and her husband Louis were in their 80s and still living independently. They both had multiple health issues, but Louis was in worse shape.

She had been the primary caregiver all her life, raising two kids and caring for her working husband. As her husband's health declined, she became the main caregiver for him. When it was too much, she had to bring help into the house. As Louis's health declined, she could not handle the extra work and the painful decision was made to put Louis in a nursing home and bring in hospice help.

Her role was changing. For her the change was an unknown.

"I feel guilty that I can't take care of him anymore," she said.

When he died, she was alone for the first time. She had to grieve. Her family was near and was there for her, but grieving was not easy.

Women and men face similar questions and guilt: What if my best is not enough to save my loved one? What if I cannot care for them anymore? How do I accept and adapt to my changing role?

The good news is that many others have gone through this tough time and survived. They did it. The idea that we can grieve, and grow is proven by the millions who lose a spouse or child every year and live to tell about it. We adapt to new roles.

We do not like the changes but when we accept that the roles are changing, we can work with those changes.

What we think of grieving can be quite different from the reality that we face. Yet we face it because we must heal ourselves and heal our loved ones. The idea is not pleasant, but it is a part of the fluidity of life.

Drowning yourself in drugs, alcohol, or risky behaviors is running away from grief. That is easy to do. That is weakness. Wanting to avoid pain is easy. However, grieving is not easy.

Accepting our loss takes strength because we must accept our weakness. Accepting pain, loneliness, and despair takes emotional strength. As we adapt to the loss and reinvent ourselves, we are taking the boldest step of all: becoming who we are—and that takes strength.

Grieving

How long do I grieve?

I thought I knew the answer to this question. I thought it was a one-year deal and that grief would be over and life would continue as normal. I had a lot to learn. I had read about death and grieving before my wife passed, and I thought grieving was a process that took a year. When my wife passed, I was told by a counselor that it would take five years to be back to where I was before my wife died.

Five years? Why so long?

Do not be shocked at the five-year time period. Grief, according to the Mayo Clinic, "...is a strong, sometimes overwhelming, emotion for people, regardless of whether their sadness stems from the loss of a loved one, or from a terminal diagnosis, they or someone they love, has received. Grieving takes time, and the amount of time is as unique as the individual."

Grief is the natural reaction to loss.

Five-years, based on my experience, was the right amount of time to work through grief and get to the point where I could look back and remember the good times and smile. It is not a precise date or a set amount of time. It was more of an acceptance that I was not in shock over the death, was adapting to my new life, felt that I was healing, and was accepting that my life was going in a new direction, and it felt right.

In the beginning of grief, individuals might find themselves feeling numb and removed from daily life, unable to carry on with regular duties while saddled with their sense of loss, fear of losing control, and disorientation.

Yes, grief is a natural reaction to loss, and it is not easy. The Mayo Clinic also says that mourning can last for months or years. Generally, the grief is tempered as time passes and as the bereaved adapts to life without their loved one. There is shock and grief to the news of a terminal diagnosis or to the notion that someone they love may die.

I found the first year an emotionally and mentally challenging year of trying to figure out what was happening to my life and why it hurt so much. I worked through shock and disbelief, anger and guilt, depression and despair. I felt like crying all the time. I slept late in the morning and did not want to fall asleep at night. Other issues I faced in that first year were my kids, their school, their activities, business and volunteer time. I stumbled and mumbled my way through these times because they were what my life had become. Yet I made it through.

Others in my first-year support group, who were on average about 20-30 years older than me, faced issues such as how to pay the bills, whom to call for home repairs, and other issues that couples faced after being together for 20 years or more.

My second year was my year of loneliness. I felt so alone. I was not dealing with the emotional shock, anger, and depression, but I was faced with the reality of being alone and dealing with feelings of frustration and resentment. This was just as bad as year one. I was in limbo because I did not know how to be me without her, but day-by-day I made it through year two. I found that grief attacks came in waves.

"With time, such emotional waves become less frequent and much less severe," says Dr. Jacks.

Emotional waves? Yes, that is a good description because grief attacks are not a constant barrage against an individual; they come and go like waves rolling onto a beach with the exception that they are not as predictable as ocean waves.

Healing is like waves too. Healing is slow but steady until life seems normal. It seemed like I was struggling in neck-deep water, but eventually I got to the shallows, then onto the shore. This is adjusting to the shock of grief and adapting to the new life and living that life.

Years 3-5 I lump together because they were the years of trying to mesh my emotional and mental life back. I had to adapt and struggle to accept the new responsibilities of young children. I also had to be part of new social networks.

The boys were now a couple of years older and they became involved in school shows, celebrations, sports, and artistic endeavors.

I had to develop new relations with parents, teachers, and school administrators. I had to put myself out in front of people that were not grieving and be me—me without my spouse, me as the professional that I had been. It was a tough act.

Each year brought some ending to a different phase of grieving. Each year the feelings of loss and loneliness became less and less. I became more focused with each passing year. It was a progression from grieving to accepting life on my own terms.

Did it take five years to recover?

Yes, the grief that came with the shock of her death is gone. I accepted what happened and had to adapt to a new way of living and relating to people. The emotions I deal with today represent today's anger, depression, and anxiety about my job and self-esteem. I can recall my late wife and I recall the grief I felt at her loss. That will always be a part of me. But I do not live in grief.

As the Mayo Clinic stated, pain is tempered as time passes. As time passed, I grieved less. I hurt less. The time between grief attacks grew longer and longer. "You will be in a different place," says Dr. Jacks. "The experience that you have gone through will help you deal with the feelings and emotions that come up."

"Grief is a process, and we go through that process at our own speed. It is very personal," says David B. Feldman, Ph.D., author, speaker, and professor of counseling psychology at Santa Clara University. It isn't a race to the finish line. Whether you are done sooner or later than someone else is just a matter of who you are rather than some timetable.

My mother died 27 years after my wife died. I grieved the loss of my mother. I also grieved for the loss of my first wife. It is all grief. It is the feeling of losing people we love. I loved them both. The feelings and thoughts of what do we do now was something I had in common with my siblings.

When you are grieving, you want the pain to end. You want to be you again. You want your life back. How long it takes depends on how old we are, what our motivation is, and working through the pain. Hard grief ends sooner rather than later. The merging of our lives takes time. You will not grieve forever. You will know how long it takes when you can look back and be thankful it is over. You will feel well again. Just take your time.

Guilt

Why do I feel guilty when I did nothing wrong?

Survivor's guilt is the guilt that people feel when they survive an experience that many others may not have survived. Sometimes that feeling is from something they did or did not do that affected the life of another. The website 'What's Your Grief', Whatsyourgrief.com, states there are many types of guilt that arise in grief. It is also very complex as it varies from person to person.

Some of us feel guilty over what we did or didn't do.

I felt guilt when my wife died. Why? Because I was still alive, and I thought there must have been more that I could have done to save her. When I look back at those times, I wonder; should I have taken her to a bigger hospital? Should I have taken her to the best cancer specialist around? Maybe I should have, but we did seek out western medical help and non-western alternative medicine. Could I have done more? Maybe, but the time is past.

According to Dr. Kathleen Nadar, survivor's guilt can come from any event where one survives. It is usually associated with war, natural disaster, and acts of violence. Many survivors of the 9/11 attacks on the twin towers felt survivor's guilt. Those who saved themselves were glad they survived but about a month later they started to have nightmares, repeated mental images of the horrors the survivor had witnessed, and other symptoms began to undermine their lives, said Nadar.

Survivor's guilt has been the subject of movies such as *Sophie's' Choice* (1982), *Ordinary People* (1980), and TV series like *Rescue Me* and *Law & Order: UK*.

What can you do if you feel guilty? Here are suggestions from the 'What's your grief' website: Know that the feelings are real and that they are yours. You are not alone. Talk to a counselor if you get stuck. Enjoy your life because you have survived. Don't get stuck on the whys. Grieve for those who died, in your way. Celebrate that you are alive and know that it does not minimize your grief for those who died.

Remember that survivor's guilt is normal. In and of itself, it isn't a sign of unhealthy grief, despite the fact that some people will make you feel like it isn't okay to feel guilty. What you go through is unique to you because of your relationship with the deceased.

Holidays

How can I make it through the holidays?

The holidays are not necessarily a happy, merry time—especially for people whose loved ones have died during the past year, or even the past several years. According to the Center for Disease Control, over 2.8 million people die each year in the US leaving millions of loved ones engulfed in grief. If you are one of the grieving, chances are the holidays only accentuate your sadness, loneliness, and sense of loss.

Are there ways to get through Christmas, Hanukkah and the New Year with minimal suffering and some level of enjoyment? Yes, there are ways to make the holidays more bearable and even pleasant.

I know this journey firsthand. My late wife was in the hospital for Thanksgiving and died ten days before Christmas. She was only 38 years old, and we had two sons under the age of seven. It made the first holiday season without her nearly unbearable. Although I walked through that first Christmas like a zombie, in subsequent years I found ways that helped me, and they could help you have a far more positive experience.

Here are my tried and true tips to get through the holidays after suffering the death of a loved one:

Turn to a hospice for help. The hospice is not only for the dying, but for the living as well (See Hospice for the Living). It provides individual and group counseling for those left behind. Some hospices even offer public seminars on how to get through the holidays.

Keep your expectations for yourself and the holidays reasonable. Do not put undue pressure on yourself by "demanding" that you act and feel a certain way. Things will be different and probably not as merry as before—at least for a while. But you can experience some degree of happiness and enjoyment. Accept where you are in the grief process.

Validate your feelings. Do not stuff them down. Cry and feel sad. But do not allow them to engulf you. Have a list of things written down that you can do that will help you feel better—watch a funny movie, listen to uplifting music, play your favorite sport, meditate, take a bubble bath, or engage in your favorite hobby.

Do something for someone else. Serve Christmas dinner at a soup kitchen or sing carols in a nursing home. Get outside of yourself and your own miseries and bring joy to others. In turn, it will bring tremendous joy to you.

Surround yourself with supportive, loving people. If you are with your family, wrap yourself in their love and care.

Give yourself a break. Do not feel like you must make the holidays happen for others. Pass the baton to someone else with zero guilt. Let someone else cook the turkey and clean up the kitchen. Be a pampered person!

Reminisce with family and friends. Talk about your loved one and share memories with others. Let laughter and happy times return as you reminisce about your loved one's life. Lead the way in talking as others might be uncomfortable.

Journal, journal, journal. Write out your feelings and thoughts; commit them to paper. It is a remarkable healing process with scientific research behind it. Journaling should be continued throughout the holidays and well beyond.

By following these tips, you can make your holiday a bit brighter. You will survive the holidays. You will be okay with the knowledge that you did it once, and you can do it again.

Holidays will bring the memories of our loved ones back because we used to enjoy the holidays with them. Now, we share the holidays with those who are left, or with new people. We can survive the holidays by keeping our expectations real, letting others into our holiday, and sharing responsibility. Share time and memories with your family or be alone. Make the holidays a time for you.

Hope

When does hope die and return?

There is always hope. That is what I have always told myself, and what I tell others. But on a cold December night, my hope died. On that cold December night, my wife died. Exhausted from the long day, shock, emotional stress, and feeling empty, I shut my eyes to the world.

That first day dragged on till evening.

Just like any evening, I put the boys in their room and talked to them, hugged them, talked to them some more until it was time for me to go to our—or my—bedroom.

I went through my normal bedtime routine and got in bed. But this night, the bed felt different. It was vastly colder, larger, and lonelier than before. Lisa had not been in this bed for three months because she was in the hospital.

This night was the first night in three months that Lisa was not alive.

Then it hit me: I had been holding on to hope, and hope was not here anymore.

The hope I had, that she would continue to live, was dead. The hope that we would have more time together was dead. The belief in her invincibility was dead. The hope of a married life lived until old age was dead. I had nothing but an aching that I had never known.

I had lost hope. I broke down and sobbed.

This was the worst I had ever felt. Yet what could I do but suffer with my pain?

My belief and hope in her living were gone. How would I ever have hope again?

Hope came when I woke up.

It was not an actual recognition of hope, but it began to build when I saw my kids and my family. It was a hope that I would see my kids grow up and recover from the loss of their mother.

Living is hoping for something new, different, or wanting something to happen. Buried under the grief and despair, there is hope but it is so hard to see it. I couldn't see it. But it was there. It carried me through the crushing days of grief to the acceptance of my loss, and to see my kids grow up.

Even if you do not have kids, hope for a day that is better than the day before. The next day will be better and you must believe and hope that it will. Because it will be better. You can give hope to others by getting up every day. By living, you give hope to people who do not know the pain you have gone through. You give hope to others that they can survive too.

Hospice

Can hospice help the living?

When people think about a hospice, they think of it as a place where you go to die. Yet, people die in hospitals, homes, assisted living facilities, on the street, and even alone. My wife died in a hospital.

A hospice is not a physical place like a hospital—it is a theory of care that seeks to minimize pain and give patients the best quality of life when there is no cure to the disease. It is a hard concept to grasp for many people.

What can a hospice do for the living?

For one, a hospice offers grief counseling.

My boys and I took advantage of a hospice's grief counseling services to help us deal with our loss. This year-long group counseling was offered at Avow Hospice. I went to their campus, and the boys took their sessions at the local elementary school. They provided this service free-of-charge too. It helped us understand and cope with what we were going through at a time when we needed understanding.

Some hospices offer other services and advice such as advanced directives on health care for the terminally ill, volunteer opportunities, music therapy, and veterans' services. Some also offer seminars and classes for caregivers and the public. The services offered depend on the hospice.

What I learned at the hospice were ways to see my situation and identify what I was going through, so I did not feel so alone or crazy. Being widowed and grieving can make you feel crazy because there are ideas of grieving that are in total opposition to what I was feeling and thinking.

I learned that there was more to the hospice than just dying. I learned the hospice philosophy of comfort care, and I learned how to cope with my grief. I learned that my hospice offered volunteer opportunities to people in the community through their thrift store and in other parts of their organization.

The hospice also offered palliative care or care for those with a serious illness. I contacted a hospice for my mother while she was alive. My mother was in assisted living and began having trouble, and we called in a hospice to help. They regulated her medications, provided the sanitary products she needed, visited her, and provided her with music therapy.

This hospice service gave my sister and me a break from caregiving. It also gave us a professional to call when we had questions or needed advice. They were there for us after mom died by offering counseling services.

My good friend was having several medical problems and had been close to death a couple of times. The last time his health declined, his family called in a hospice. They started his care with a review of his medications. After several months on hospice care, he graduated. This means that his health improved so much that he did not need hospice care anymore. He graduated from the hospice over 7 years ago, and he is still going strong.

Hospice nurses work with the terminally ill. They make house calls to people who are living at home with a spouse as a caregiver, or a paid caregiver. They check on their patients like a nurse in a hospital would do, except the patients are not all in one place.

The hospice helped with grief counseling. They helped my friend live longer. They gave comfort to my mother in the last 5 months of her life. They help patients with medical needs who choose to live at home, or are in hospitals, nursing home or other facilities.

According to Angela Morrow, RN., writing for the website verywellhealth.com, and at the time of this writing, people seeking hospice services can have the services provided by Medicare. There are four levels of care: Routine home care, continuous home care, inpatient care, and respite care. Your doctor must follow the Medicare guidelines for each area.

Hospices help the living in so many ways—by offering counseling, respite care, care of our family members coping with losses, and helping those in pain live longer too. The hospice was there for my sons and me, my sister and me, and our friends. When you do not know what you need, consult your doctor, and ask about hospice care to help you.

Hurtful words

What words hurt a person in grief?

When our loved one dies, the emotions and feelings can be overwhelming. People are well-meaning as they try to offer words of comfort. According to the article 'What they meant to say: looking beyond hurtful comments in grief' by Eleanor Haley, MS and program Director at the 'What's your grief' website, there are some people who always know the right thing to say. "On the other end of the spectrum, some people are consistently terrible. They carelessly say and do stupid things without giving their behavior a second thought. Some people simply aren't comfortable with grief."

People tried to say the right things to me after my wife died. I know they were trying to help me, but when I was grieving, the words were hurtful. Phrases such as 'You will find someone new', 'They are in a better place,' 'It's God's will', or 'They were needed elsewhere," hurt.

These phrases are meant to help on a deeper level, but right after the loss, they seemed cold and insulting because I was in so much pain that I could not even think about the deeper level. That deeper level of thought came later with the passage of time.

The website Funeral Guide, states that "Bereavement is a difficult, lonely time, but negative attitudes and hurtful words from those around you can make it even more difficult to cope. But grief can make even the most well-intentioned remark feel like a painful attack, and sometimes, unfortunately, people might not know when they hurt you."

People do not intend to be mean. They are trying, in their own way, to give you comfort in your loss. They may not know the right words to say, especially if they have never lost someone close. If they are actually intending to be mean, then you should reconsider having such a negative person in your life.

At times of grief, you want supportive and understanding people, and those who can listen to you without judgment. Those people let you grieve your way. When you are faced with the death of a loved one, it is a tough time of your life. Understand that not everyone will have the best words to say, but they want the best for you.

Intimacy

Can I be intimate again?

Contrary to popular belief, intimacy is NOT purely physical, says the website eHarmony. You do not have to be sexually involved with someone to be intimate with them. Instead, intimacy is a connection that builds between two people over time. Emotional closeness, spiritual trust, and physical connectedness all play a role in creating intimacy. "The causes of behavior and human experience (are) complex and include elements that are biological, psychological, social, contextual, and even spiritual," states Lori H. Gordon, Ph.D., founder of the pioneering psycho-educational PAIRS(R) program.

"There are many types of love," says Dr. Jacks. "And we grieve our losses on a different level depending on the depth of our relationship. When a person who died was a spouse or significant other, the loss of intimacy can seem unbearable." When my wife died, I felt the intimacy bonds break, both physical and emotional.

As a man, I confused sex with intimacy.

I thought I wanted sex, but what I was looking for was intimacy. The kind of intimacy I had with my wife. The kind of intimacy that is a knowing look or a soft hand to hold. Sex could be boring but not the person you are with.

It was the intimacy, the emotional and thoughtful part of me that was searching for help—searching for that feeling of connectedness where sex is the expression of our emotional love. After her death, we didn't have that physical connectedness anymore, but I still had the emotional connectedness of intimacy.

This subject is difficult to write about because I must admit my mistakes, weaknesses, and failures in dealing with women and in dealing with my own emotions, wants and needs. After my wife died, when my grief and loss were the hardest, I sought physical intimacy under the mistaken assumption that it would lead to the acceptance and love that I had lost. It didn't.

It was not just physical intimacy that I was seeking. I needed and longed for the intimacy of security, love, and protection from the real world that I had with my late wife. I needed to feel loved. I needed to feel like me again. I needed to feel.

But as a man, that type of neediness is seen as a sign of weakness. What I wanted was an emotional, intimate relationship like the one I had before the death of my wife. The emotional wanting is seen as a sign of weakness. It isn't. In fact, it is a sign of our humanity.

A physical relationship is easy to be in too. A touch was a feeling, and I wanted to feel something other than hurt and grief. If the body is working, then it is easy. Plus, the physical relation seems more like a couple's relation. But I had no partner. I was missing the feelings of relationship and I had abandonment issues as pointed out by Fran Fritscher in her article "Fear of Intimacy: Signs, Causes, and Coping Strategies" on the Very Well Mind website.

I thought that a physical relation would lead to the emotional intimacy that I wanted. I was wrong. Yet physical contact was a way for me to have some feeling, which made me feel alive. It led to some healing but not total healing because I was afraid of showing my true self like Fritscher wrote about. My true self was what my wife saw and what a few close friends saw.

According to Seth Myers, Psy.D., men score higher on a Fear-of-intimacy Scale and antidotal events point to men having a higher fear of intimacy. Additionally, he says that "...men who are afraid of relationships may have had a previous relationship as an adult that was traumatic. Having a previous partner who abused them in any way, cheated on them, left them, or died can cause these men to later avoid emotional intimacy and relationships altogether. Though some or all of these men may still have a desire for closeness, the emotional pain from the previous trauma is too great for these men to take the risk and jump into a relationship again."

I was avoiding emotional intimacy even though I was searching for it like Myers said. The emotional intimacy I was searching for was too hard to accept because of the pain of losing Lisa. For me, it was not an easily solved issue. I had experienced hard grieving and I was not eager to feel it again.

Physical relationships are easier: There is no emotional attachment. I could hide my fears. I made this mistake over and over until I figured it out. It took me a long time to realize and accept that what I was doing was wrong. You must give yourself time to heal and not fulfill someone else's timetable.

"Intimacy issues can linger for a long time," says Dr. Jacks. "Be gentle with yourself."

When I realized I was hiding my emotions, and avoiding being myself, I resolved to change my way of dating and relating to women. If what I was doing was not getting me to where I wanted to be, then I had to change. The change took time because as one issue was resolved, another issue was revealed. There were mistakes but the outcome I was looking for was achieved: I was able to open myself and let women in to know the true me. I opened myself to rejection, abandonment, and was able to be vulnerable.

Over time and through many relationships and analyzing my emotional response, I came to understand what emotional closeness was all about. I was able to open myself up, and close myself off, when needed. I learned to trust and be emotionally vulnerable again.

Facing my fears, I was able to open myself up to accept what I had been through and to be open again for true intimacy. The changes I made changed who I dated, and how I related to new people. I was ready, even facing grief possibilities again, but I was ready. When the right woman walked into my life and I wanted to make a commitment, I was able to be intimate on an emotional, spiritual, intellectual, and physical level.

Intimacy happens on many levels with couples as they grow together. Death tears apart that intimacy. We, the survivors, widows, and widowers, must rebuild ourselves. Our commitment to intimacy is a commitment to heal and establish the openness that we once had. Working to be open is hard work but it makes us ready to enter a new relationship, if that is what we choose. Only you know if that is right for you. You can do it.

Journaling

How can journaling help?

Anyone who has lost a loved one knows all too well the challenges involved in facing the reality and finality of that death. Inexplicably, the loss is compounded when guilt, depression, and despair often overwhelm those left behind. Grief takes on the proportions of a tsunami with the power to devastate a life—at least that is how it feels when grief is new and beyond measure. What can you do to weather the storm? You can either tie yourself to a tree, brace for the impact like islanders have been known to do in order to survive a tsunami or run as fast as you can in the other direction in an attempt to evade and escape.

Will it be the tree and rope approach or running for your life? Confront or repress? The odds of outrunning a tsunami are slim to none. Grief *can* be repressed over the short term. But be assured that repression will not get you where you want to go since it only sublimates grief and most definitely does not eliminate it. Like a beach ball being held under water, it will eventually pop back up to give us an opportunity to confront it and work through it. Like it or not, confronting and dealing with grief provides the way to live again. So, grab a rope, pick out a worthy tree and brace for the impact.

When death does invade your life, the best advice one can follow is to give grief expression, acknowledgement, and go through the often-painful recovery process. Grief cannot and should not be denied. Fully confronting grief is critical if you want to heal after suffering a loss. Tamping down, denying grief, and running from it only delays the healing process. Failing to talk about it and express your heartfelt feelings only postpone the inevitable and increase the depth and duration of suffering.

Journaling can be done anywhere, takes less time than a cup of coffee, it is free, and best of all, it has been scientifically proven to improve how we process issues that compromise one's quality of life so says Dr. Pennebaker, a Regents Centennial Professor of Liberal Arts and Professor of Psychology at the University of Texas at Austin. He is a social psychologist and author.

Recognizing your own deep feelings and allowing your grief to be expressed will make all the difference in the world. Share with a trusted friend and keep a journal of your thoughts and feelings. Seek help from a professional if you are not making progress. Working with a hospice counselor or grief therapist can be tremendously beneficial.

Pennebaker also says "One of the brain's functions is to help us understand events in our lives. Writing helps construct a narrative to contextualize trauma and organize ideas. Until we do this, the brain replays the same non-constructive thought patterns over and over, and we become stuck. Writing about grief and trauma helps achieve closure which tells the brain its work is done. This closure frees us, enabling us to move forward."

I journaled my loss. That journal became my award-winning book, *Life without Lisa.* Publishing your feelings is not the end goal for everyone. As a writer, that is what I did. My goal behind having my journal published was to help others.

Being able to talk and write about what you are going through and how you feel will yield positive results. Even though it seems impossible, expressing grief brings acceptance, healing and charts the course for you living a happy life again. You will amazingly survive the onslaught and be able to untie yourself from the tree to go forward to forge a new life.

Use a journal to give words to your deepest feelings, anguish, hopes and seemingly impossible dreams. Confront and face the tsunami head-on. You will survive. Generously give yourself time to heal and allow for the seemingly improbable promise of a new, happy tomorrow.

"Journaling became a safe place for me to not only write down words, but also to draw pictures as a healthy outlet for my sometimes-overwhelming emotions," said Jenny Wheeler, an author who wrote a book about grieving as a teenager.

Embrace the process. Expect miraculous healing. Look toward a new tomorrow. Writing down your thoughts and feelings gets them out of you and onto paper. Looking at those words helps your mind in many ways. Your journal is for your eyes only, and only you decide what happens to it. You can publish it, save it, burn it, or delete it. It is up to you. The journal is a tool for you to use to actively participate in your healing. Write freely and often.

Living

What is living again?

"When a loss happens, the thought—or lack of thought—about living occurs. We go through the motions for the sake of those still living and for the deceased. It is common to feel like you can't go on, and that you do not want to live," said Dr. Gloria Horsley, PhD., in a talk with Dr. Howard R. Winokuer, Ph.D., LPC, NCC, on an Open to Hope podcast.

How can we live without our dead spouse? How do we live after our loss? Most of the time, people stumble though life after a loss. Sometimes we do not want to go on living. Dr. Winokuer said that one of the most important decisions we can make is to go on living. It is a conscious decision that even though we suffered a loss, our life is important and that we want to live.

For me, I knew that I had a long life to live. But I did not know how to do that after Lisa died. I could not think of life as being normal. The first two things I did were what I had done when Lisa was alive—which was working out and ballroom dancing. But I had to be convinced to do it. I could not do it on my own.

My friend Ray convinced me to go to the gym with him. So, I started going to the gym. Ray and his girlfriend were taking ballroom dance lessons and he encouraged me to come to a studio where he was learning, so that I could dance too.

These were the first steps in getting back to living. Then came the activities that took place when my kids went to elementary school. I had to be there for them, the teachers, and the administration.

These activities were the start of my living again. Lisa's life had ended but my life continued. As Dr. Winokuer said, "that once you are able to accept that it is your life you are living, then the ability to go beyond what you had done in the past and do more."

I looked at my life, how short the time with Lisa was, and that my life could be cut short too. I made the decision to live.

I had always wanted to learn to ride a motorcycle. I had a bike when I was 16, and it was a cheap bike. It only ran one day, and I wiped out. I did not know how to control the bike. At forty-nine, I saw an ad for motorcycle rider education. I jumped at the chance. I learned to ride a motorcycle. I bought a bike and I have taken short trips and long trips up to 2,000 miles in a week.

I was always fascinated by planes. I went to the small, local airport that offered flying lessons and I started learning how to operate a plane. The first few lessons gave me a great view of the world, but my inner ear problems kicked in and I had to lay flat for a week. I started again and racked up over one hundred hours of flight time before I stopped.

I put my kids into self-defense class to learn jiujitsu. I liked what they were learning so I took classes for a couple of years.

I took piano lessons, guitar lessons, and learned to shoot a pistol. I even learned how to replace a toilet. I felt fearless. I wanted to live as much as possible and learn as much as possible. It didn't mean I would be proficient or get a degree or license in the subject. I studied for my personal knowledge and satisfaction.

I joined Kiwanis, a community-based group of volunteers helping improve the lives of children in our community. It is there that I learned about my leadership ability and the ability to speak in public.

I learned about business through books, seminars, online classes, and even earned my MBA at age sixty. I took personal improvement group classes and therapy sessions to learn how to open up after grief and be present.

Time is limited, and after the death of a loved one, we learn the value of time. Our loved one is not alive anymore, but we are. We also learn to accept that life is short, and we may not have much time left. Choosing to live is a conscience decision. We live just like our spouses would have wanted us to live. Choose to live and fulfill all the dreams that you can in your life.

Memorials

What type of memorial should I have?

According to the website 'Dignity Funerals', memorials can include cremation memorials, plaques, benches, headstones, vases, statues, trees, jewelry, and mausoleums. There is also the obituary in the newspaper, markers of where our bodies lay, or something in remembrance for all to see.

What are memorials for? Memorials are physical evidence that someone once had a physical existence here on Earth says the website Good Funeral Guide. It keeps that person in mind, and perpetuates their memory. It remains an enduring point of contact with them, a place where you can go and talk to them. The type of memorial you choose can be anything as cited above.

Memorials can be private or public. The choice is up to you.

For my late wife I chose a headstone to mark her burial site. The obituary appeared in the paper. I did not plant a tree, or erect benches, or vases and statues. I do not have a wall of pictures or light candles. I felt that my choice was traditional.

The cemetery where my late wife is buried has a host of monuments to remember the deceased. Simple stones, statues, ornate markers. Some had poems, some pictures or carvings. Our stone has an etching of a lighthouse. My parents' stone has a carving of a motorboat, which my dad loved.

There are also roadside memorials to remember where people had been killed in car crashes. There are sidewalk memorials where people want to remember the famous and not so famous people in their lives.

We all want to remember our loved ones. We go to a space where our loved one's physical body was last present. We attach ourselves to the last place the physical body was at because the invisible remembrances are too complex to share.

In the first year or two, I did things to remember her, such as light candles on her birthday, or arrange a cake or flowers. As the years passed and the kids grew older, life brought on new issues, and I did not observe her death anniversary. I didn't celebrate her birthday, and then our wedding day. Those were the invisible memorials that I remembered.

In this electronic age, there are funeral home pages of those who have died. We can search nationwide for people we may know. People post memorials on Facebook. They post on the death anniversary of their loved one. They memorialize their loved ones on their page. It is not something I did or would do now. I can see why people post memories of the love they lost, but I have a hard time wanting to do that.

But posting on Facebook, or other social media, is not what I chose to do.

Many on Facebook did not even know my late wife. They never met her. They only know me and my current wife. When people get to know me, they will learn about my late wife. Is it cold of me to not post a memorial to her or erect a large monument to our love? Maybe, but I prefer to remember her and memorialize her in many ways. Ways that are unique to me and who she was.

I set up a scholarship in my late wife's name to help nursing students. That is my memorial. The fund is named after her and her profession and is administered by the university. It helps college students now. It will help them in the future. Every year there is a student who receives financial assistance from her scholarship fund. I have a scholarship set up in my name, at a different university, where a student will receive my funds and I will be remembered.

I know people who have set up charitable foundations in memory of family members who died senselessly and who want to prevent the deaths of other.

We can set up memorials of grave markers, benches, vases, urns, Facebook posts, and scholarships. The memorials can be serious or not. We want our loved ones remembered. We want a place we can go to connect with the dead and remember their lives. A memorial gives us something physical that we can go to and remember. The choice of what type of memorial, and how many, is up to you.

Memories

How do I create new and happy memories?

Memories are interesting. We can make them. We can lose them, forget them, reimagine them, and we can make new ones.

When I was first widowered, the memories of my wife were not just in my mind, they were everywhere in our house. There were pictures on the walls, clothing, furniture, and of course, the kids. There was no getting around the fact that she was there.

We built memories together, over years of living. We never thought of our lives as a living memory or building memories. We were too busy raising the kids.

After she passed, I started creating new memories with the kids. They needed new and pleasant memories to remember. I started taking them to places their mom and I had never been to. This was good for building memories as a family of three, as well as for making new memories that I needed too.

I wanted memories of just me because it was just me—the single adult. It was part of establishing my single life as a man, not just as a widower. Would I and did I want to remember my widowhood? At first, I could not think of the past at all.

As I dated, I started creating new memories with the women I dated. Eventually, I did remarry, and the topic of building memories came up. In my new marriage, I chose to repress the memories of the women I had dated because they were not in my life just like the memory of my late wife. They were in my past, and I did not need to remember them in my marriage.

According to the website Family Education, new memories for second marriages can include starting a new photo album and keeping it out on your bookshelves, finding a new favorite restaurant, creating special traditions all your own, and/or choosing art for your walls together. Over time, replace your daily-use kitchen items that you used during your previous marriage, and carefully wrap and store all valuable wedding gifts from your previous marriage too.

This does not imply forgetting your late loved one. It is moving on in life with a new relationship that needs new things that you both agree upon.

My new wife, Terri, and I, decided we wanted to have memories that were uniquely ours. These memories did not involve my late wife or her ex-husband. We consciously decided to make happy memories to carry us into the future. We decided that we would create new memories in our travel choices. We deliberately decided to go to places that each of us had wanted to visit but had never gone to with our spouses. And sometimes the mode of travel was different too.

I started riding a motorcycle at age 49. Riding had been a lifelong dream of mine. My wife had ridden on motorcycles in the past, and she always imagined going on long trips but never had. For our honeymoon, we talked about going to Italy and the rest of Europe, but we had done that with our previous spouses. We decided to see United States state parks and natural land formations that neither of us had seen. We decided to see them on my 2004 BMW 1150RT motorcycle.

We spent 11 days riding from Rapid City, South Dakota, into northern Wyoming, and looping back through southern Wyoming into Nebraska, and back to Rapid City.

The first day out, the rain pounded us. We stopped and had pie and coffee at a Perkins restaurant until the rain let up. We visited Mt. Rushmore and Devil's Tower. We took a hundred-mile detour to avoid flooded areas in southeast Wyoming. As tourists, we went horseback riding, hiked, and dug for dinosaur bones. We saw buffalo, the Crazy Horse statue in progress, and soaked in the natural hot springs of Thermopolis, WY. It was the coolest stuff. Neither of us had done anything like this before, and I got to do it with my wife. It was a great trip. But much more than a great trip, it is a great memory.

Dr. Harley, a Ph.D. and a Licensed Clinical Psychologist, says when our marriage provides us with a recreational activity that we both enjoy, an anchor memory, that creates an enjoyable memory and a great marriage. The more activities that we enjoy with each other, the more positive our love and life will be

The first 4 years of happiness of my previous marriage was interrupted by 4 years of disease that helped to create the disease memories. I wanted to forget the disease memories and replace them with happy memories.

When my late wife and I moved to Florida, we set up our house, but she never lived there. It was a bachelor pad that the boys and I inhabited. It had that manly touch, look, and feel to it like the big screen TV, masculine colors, and the lack of a feminine presence.

The next issue in my second marriage was where to live. Terri moved into my house, and we started to update it. It was the process of her turning the bachelor pad into our house. The process was creating memories for us—for how we melded our styles to create our house. But it got to the point where it was still too much of a bachelor pad. We decided to move to a new house: a neutral house for all our kids and family.

Whether you change small items or large ones, you will create new memories of your life as it goes forward. This is not replacing or forgetting the past but building on your life and creating happy memories with the partner you love.

A memory can be anything you do with your new spouse or partner. Memories come in many forms, like how a person talks, gestures, smiles, laughs, or what you do with that person. Those memories will always be with you. You can remember and recall past events and people at any time. You will not forget.

In the present, after the trauma, I chose to create new memories—new memories of happy times with a new person. You can create new memories too. Memories are very fluid. I hope you choose to make happy memories for the rest of your life.

Memories

When to share memories?

Sharing can be challenging. What do you share about your grief? Do you share details of who your past loved one was with new friends or anyone? And what about the people who do not want you to share? In the tangled time of grieving, expressing or repressing can be challenging.

In the first year of grief, it was hard for me to share my stories of my late wife because the pain was raw. I could share memories with my friends because we had those shared memories. Some people did not understand that I was not emotionally strong enough to share stories of our past life. But I wanted people to remember her.

"Knowing when it's appropriate to reminisce and when it might cause more pain for the bereaved can be challenging," says Dr. Jacks.

There were many times when I didn't want to talk about Lisa. I did not want to remember the loss. Sometimes I just wanted to sit in silence and not talk about her or remember the past.

But there was one thing I was certain of: I wanted our friends to talk and remember her. I told them that even though Lisa is dead, I would still talk about her. I expected my friends to talk about her too.

They should not be worried about mentioning her because it may cause me pain. I was already in pain and if they chose to ignore her, it would hurt me even more. I would feel that it was a denial of her life and our life together. I did not want my life denied. Our life had meaning. It was special. It is the kids' history too. I did not shy away from talking about her to them.

Yet, as recovery from grief took place, I shared less because there came a point where there was no need to share. There was no need to share or remember because I was living a new life with new people in it. They did not know my past life. My late wife would occasionally come up in conversions, and people were pleased that I talked about her too. They were getting to know me without her. Yet, they wanted to know the mother of my boys too. It was then that I started to share, so that people knew our history better.

This new life became the topic of conversation and sharing as memories were built with new friends. It was moving forward with new memories with friends and leaving behind the old memories.

This is not to say I will forget my spouse or that my friends might forget her. It means that 'living' is taking place and that is what is going to be talked about. References to past events certainly come up and mentioning our deceased loved ones would be appropriate. That is fine. That is sharing.

Just as high school friends, past dates, and the kids' school mates fade into my memory, so do the memories and experiences I had with my late spouse. It is just the natural progression of living. The memories of our past loved ones can be recalled, but they have less relevance on the life we are living now. We have the memories. We share when it is appropriate or when we need to say something about our past.

Today I share with my friends what is going on now. We occasionally reminisce about the past when we were young and foolish, and the people we knew back then, but do not weep anymore. We lose friends too.

A friend of ours lost her 30-year-old daughter to a drunk driver. She needed to hear that her late daughter mattered. She wanted to share what her late daughter did in her life. We now talk with her about her late daughter because she needs validation of the fact that she had a daughter. It is sharing with her the lives of our children, mine, hers, and my new wife's child. We all have memories to share.

When sharing, you can always ask the grieving person if they want to share. Some people need to talk about their deceased loved ones. Some people cannot move past the death of a loved one and talk about them, or they have new lives and that is what they want to talk about.

If we dwell on the death, grief, and loss, then we aren't accepting the loss and are not healing from the loss. Remembering the good times will then be impossible. Remembering is good. It validates our past relationship when we can share them with friends who also remember the event.

If you are a friend of a person who has lost someone then let them lead the discussion and not be afraid to remember the deceased too if the subject is relevant. You were their friend, and you suffered a loss also.

Each of us makes a judgment about when to talk about the deceased and when the appropriate time is to talk. Our loved ones are a part of our past and when we need to share, our memories are there. With time the fond memories take over. That is a blessing to all. When we talk about past events, we can share our memories about our past loved ones, just like everyone else reminisces.

Mother's Day

How do I celebrate without the kid's mom around?

Mother's Day recalls all things maternal—warm and wonderful hugs, children's homemade cards, a delicious dinner, mom's loving kisses and smiles. Mother's Day can be extremely challenging for children who have lost a mother; not to mention school days of celebration.

I know the challenge of responding to those days. My wife died a week before Christmas when our kids were 6 and 5. Mother's Day came awfully fast for me and my two sons.

I knew my young elementary school children would obviously have to celebrate the day in ways far different from other children. I gave a lot of thought to what would help my sons get through their first Mother's Day, and others, in the best, least painful way possible. Together, we figured out approaches that worked best for them and me, but it took some thinking and doing.

I can recommend the following five approaches to help you and your kids celebrate Mother's Day, if they do not have a mother present in their lives. I hope these tips help you too.

Remember the good times. Pictures are great for triggering memories. Bring them out and talk to your kids about the day each picture was taken. Share the life you and your wife were dreaming about and how she felt about having kids. Keep the talk on an age-appropriate level. There will be days to come when they are older and can understand more. Always reassure them that you and they are a team, and you have no intention of breaking up the team.

Establish new routines. A new routine can be simple or elaborate. On the first Mother's Day after my wife died, I bought roses. The kids and I went to the local pier and threw the roses into the Gulf of Mexico. Yes, we looked out of place in our Sunday best among the swimsuit set, but we were on a mission. The boys enjoyed participating in this unique tribute to their beloved mother. Find your special place for your new routine.

Find a "new mom" for the children to honor. This doesn't mean getting married right away. It means finding a mom substitute—a sister, aunt, grandmother, or special female friend to whom your young children can send cards and write messages. This helps remove the stigma of being a motherless child in elementary or middle school. My boys chose their Aunt Stephanie and my mother.

Encourage your kids to write a letter to their mom. When having kids write such a letter, make sure they know it is for them and their mom only and that no one else will read it. You might want to put the letters in an envelope for safekeeping. If the kids are open to it, you can read the previous year's letter before writing a new one. You can save their letters and return them when they are older.

Eat cake. Go to a movie or rent a movie. Kids do not want to sit and grieve. They do not want to sit, period. Get up and get out of the house. Shoot basketballs, throw a baseball, play miniature golf, or go to a zoo. Enjoy a new day. Create positive new memories to crowd out the negative ones.

Remind them that even though their mother is not physically around, they still have a mother who loves them dearly.

If your children are in elementary school, remember there often is a Mother's Day card-making activity at school and conversations about moms. It can be a hard time for them. Discuss with them ahead of time who they will make cards for, and hint at what to say.

Being a parent is difficult and challenging. Being a single parent with young kids is hard. Help your kids make it through Mother's Day by trying new approaches to handle a tough situation. Try new routines to create positive memories, discuss their school's Mother's Day activities and what they can do or say, have a female role model they can look up to. Talk to their teachers so they know your kid's situation.

Both my sons and I survived Mother's Day without their mom. Try these 5 tips with your children to see if they help you. We adjusted and adapted to our new way of celebrating. I assure you that you and your children can do it too.

New spouse

How do I relate to a new spouse?

Whether to marry again or not is a personal decision that depends on your age, activity level, desire to have someone in your life again, and whether you need to have someone in your life or not. There are also many issues to consider as an older adult.

For me, widowered at age 39, I wanted to marry again. I know widows and widowers who thought the opposite. My mother was widowed at age 69. She did not remarry and lived as an active single woman for the next 26 years. My new mother-in-law to-be was widowed at 83, and she did not remarry

My uncle was widowed at 70. He remarried but his second wife died when he was 76, and he then remained single.

Only you know when it is right to remarry.

Some women I dated said I should have married sooner. Maybe I should have. After grieving, I was enjoying being single. Dating alone did not get me closer to marriage, it brought me closer to who I was, and that took years of work. I had to change me, and the way I was dating and what I was looking for. I had to be open. When I was ready to share who I was and be open, I found the right woman.

I remarried at age 60.

My kids were out of the house, and her daughter was graduating from high school. We had to adjust and work together to protect our kids and blend our families (See Blended families.)

According to Dr. Nancy Kalish writing in Psychology Today, "There are so many changes and so many compromises. Some issues that are small to one person may be very important to the other. Examples from seniors I spoke to who were beginning late-life marriages included… wedding rings, photos, houses, furniture, pets, television watching, sounds, paying pills, sex, food, religion, and late spouse."

Yes, there were adjustments. My house, a bachelor pad for 20 years, and her house, were sold so we could have a neutral place to live and for the kids to come visit.

I now had a stepdaughter in my life.

My wife now had stepsons in her life.

We had to adjust to having more kids and figure out how to relate to them and love them for who they are and how they live.

I had to adjust to having a wife again. This meant taking her schedule and feelings into consideration all the time. She had her dreams and demands on her new husband too.

With all these questions and issues of a second marriage, we became a team.

It was not just about me anymore. I had to learn what being in a relationship really meant. Yes, I was married before and I knew all about that relationship. However, even though this relationship had similar circumstances, my new wife was different. I had to adjust to her outlook, and her ways of taking care of the house, shopping, and her independence.

Yes, I remarried, and I am happy that I did. I have a wife again. I have a partner to share in the household chores. I have a partner to share the special looks, winks, and laughs, and we enjoy our new routines and activities. We can talk about our kids, as we feel they are all ours.

Marriage after a loss is not for everyone. It depends on your age and interests, your interest in having a partner, and your health and your potential partner's health, and all day-to-day issues that must be solved. As we age, life changes us, and we may not want to bother with marriage again. But if you feel you want to, then go ahead. Find your next life partner. It is okay to enjoy life again with a partner who will bring joy and family to your life.

Overwhelmed

Why am I easily overwhelmed?

Before Lisa and I married, and after we married, we used to do home remodeling projects together such as wallpapering and painting, insulating walls, putting up sheetrock, and replacing or sanding floors. We did this to make money and to improve our own home. We eventually got to the point where the jobs were too big for us and we hired contractors to do the improvements, like adding additions or re-roofing the house.

That all changed after Lisa died.

Not only was my wife and home improvement partner gone, but tasks became more difficult to accomplish.

After the funeral and burial, we went back to Florida. My parents, and my father-in-law, Carl, came with us. They went shopping and bought two televisions and two fiberboard TV stands that needed assembly. So, I had a job to do. No big deal for an experienced handyman.

The television stands were several pieces of fiberboard that needed to be screwed together. I sat on the floor with all the pieces. I was fitting the screws into the predrilled holes when I turned toward to my right to say something to Lisa.

In a split-second, I realized I had forgotten that Lisa wasn't here anymore. She would have been here if she were alive. We shared so many projects together, like painting, insulating, and repairing walls and floors. My breathing became faster and deeper as I fought with the emotions that were crawling up my throat. This is crazy, I thought. I'm going to burst if I do not get out of here. I dropped the tools and went for a walk.

When Lisa and I were doing projects around the house, she and I always talked. She was not here for today's project and I realized that she is never going to be around for future projects.

Here was a simple task and I could not do it without breaking down.

That is how it was and will be. The simplest things were not so simple anymore.

"The struggle to complete tasks and make decisions is a common effect of grief," says Dr. Jacks.

I also had difficulty working with my computer, which I did not have before. My family assumed I knew everything about the house we had just moved into when I was trying to figure it out too. I was trying to be a good parent—trying to not forget how and when to cook and to notice if the kids were sick or not.

I felt stupid and incompetent at performing the simple task of putting those TV tables together. I lost my appetite, but the kids did not.

Just trying to stay current with regular, normal household issues and parenting caused many situations to be out of the ordinary. And sometimes the ordinary tasks like cleaning the house and cooking easily overwhelmed me.

As the years passed and everything was not so new, I was better able to perform as a single parent. Projects did not seem overwhelming either and I looked forward to working around the house.

Even though I was easily overwhelmed in the beginning, I found that as time passed and grief receded in my life, I was able to function normally. The routine chores of shopping, bill paying, and even home improvement projects, became easy tasks that I could do.

I could handle the emotions of loss and was able to handle my life. There were times when I did feel overwhelmed—that is typical for single parents. I took a deep breath, calmed down, and was able to focus again.

Personal items

How do I separate from personal items?

Separating from personal items is not just for widow and widowers. Anyone who has lived with another person and lost that mate, or a child, parent, partnership, or even a business, will go through a period of having to deal with the departed person's personal items.

According to Dr. Diana Jacks, "There is no magic timetable for parting with personal items." She states that the bereaved person must set their own timetable. Some people act quickly, and others take time.

According to the website 'What's Your Grief' on sorting through belongings, it says to prioritize what you tackle and if you have a business, that would be a priority, as there are bills to pay, insurance forms to fill, and bank accounts to handle. My late wife Lisa had a business. Her partners took care of the business. For me, it was the non-business personal items that were my concern.

There were her clothes, pictures, household items that she had bought, the knick-knacks that she loved, gifts she gave to me, and I to her. And just the ordinary, everyday items she used, that I observed but never really thought about, but now had to decide what to do with them.

The thought of handling those items in the first few months after her death was too much for me.

The questions were where and how to begin. What's Your Grief says that it is good to prioritize what needs to be removed first. We had moved, but I still owned the other house, so I only physically handled her items in the summer when I came back to the house. And because I did not live in the house, it gave me time for separation from her items.

I started five months after she passed.

Many people do not have that luxury. They have to live with the items every day. Though some of these items may be comforting says What's Your Grief, many are just small and painful reminders of the absence in the house.

I decided to start with items that would never be used by anyone, and the least painful to me. The first things to go were her undergarments. They were personal to Lisa but held little interest to me without her, and no one would ever use them. I threw those items away without any guilt.

The next items I picked were the four or five pocketbooks that she had left on the floor of the closet. I thought these would be easy because they were something she used, and I would never use.

I opened the first pocketbook and found photos, the coins she casually tossed in after shopping, the cellophane from cigarette packages, tissues, IDs, notes, and such. Each item brought back strong memories because I could see her with the pocketbook and see her taking things in and out of them. It was natural for her to do this and it is what I remember. I had to stop after the second one and lay on the floor from emotional exhaustion. How could a pocketbook get me so low? It brought her back to life in the small things she did every day.

I knew I had to give myself more distance from them. I eventually was able to sort through the items in each pocketbook and keep what I wanted before I threw them and the non-emotional items out.

The next to go were her shoes. Most were worn out and not in good shape. Those I tossed. There were good ones, and those I donated.

Just after her death I stared into the clothes closet and remembered her wearing each suit, dress, pants, tops, sweaters and more. I would hug them, smell her perfume that still lingered there, and remember our lives together. It was three years after her passing that I faced the clothing again.

This time I stared into the closet and saw women's clothes. Clothes I would never wear, and no other women I knew would wear. But what to do with them? They were still good. I was talking to a neighbor and she suggested a women's shelter or clothing exchange.

I found a clothing exchange for women reentering the workforce. I thought this was appropriate as Lisa had been a businesswoman. I gathered all her clothes from three house closets and filled my car, front and back seats, with the clothes, some still in the dry cleaners' plastic bag. It made me feel good that the clothes were going to help women who needed it and that Lisa was still making a difference even after her death.

The other items in the bedroom were the decorations, pictures, colors, etc., that were a reflection of her taste. The question was what did I want to keep or what did I want to change? I had a nice wooden box about eighteen inches square, and into that box I threw cards and small memorabilia to remind me of her, our wedding, and our life. I kept the small knickknacks that I liked, saved some for the kids, and put the rest out in the yard sale pile or into the trash.

Because I lived away and did not visit the house for any great length of time, it gave me time to emotionally separate from items. As the years passed, I rented rooms in the house to friends who needed a place to live. I would visit the house and paint rooms and go through the items that were left and toss more items out. Separating from her items and the house was a long-drawn-out process.

After 10 years the only items of hers that were left were a bathrobe and her wedding veil. The bathrobe I threw out; I kept the wedding veil.

When I sold the house, I moved the pieces of furniture I wanted to keep to my summer house and left what I did not want. Eventually, those items went to the kids for their homes.

One of my aunts gave away her second husband's clothing quickly. Maybe her experience with her first husband's death made it easier. I do not know. My mother only kept a few things after my dad's death. My siblings and I all got something from their house as she downsized her living space.

Separating from your deceased's possessions is winnowing down of items that are most special and important to you, within the space you must keep them.

When we remarried, my wife and I had to decide what items to keep from our respective households. I had my stuff, she had her stuff, and eventually we accumulated her parents' bedroom set and my mother' photographs.

Are you still in the same house or apartment? How about repainting it? Using the same furniture or getting new? Did you move? Is your new place yours alone? Did you have to move and make decisions quickly or did you have time?

Only you can decide when you are ready to separate from possessions. It is your grief process, and you take it at your speed. You decide what to keep, give away, or throw out. It is okay to keep items that make you feel comfortable. Do not be pressured by what other people say. The relationship you had with your loved one is unique and what you keep should reflect that. The process can be overwhelming but prioritize what is most important and what is least important and start there. Give yourself time if you can.

Photographs

How photographs can hurt or help?

Photographs, pictures, images, jpegs, etc., are all forms of captured images of our life. All these devices do the same thing: they freeze a moment in time. Those images, when we look at them, spark our memories of the time and what we were doing at that time. For those who have lost a loved one, pictures can hurt, but eventually they can heal too.

I used film cameras, then digital cameras, then cell phones to capture my images.

As an author, I speak to groups about grief and overcoming the loss. After one talk, an elderly widower approached me.

"I can't look at my wife's photographs," he said. "Is that normal?"

"How long has it been?" I asked.

"Three months," he said.

When I reminisced about the time when I had been widowered three months, I remembered that I could not look at my pictures either. At the time when he asked me that question, it had been six years since my wife had passed.

"Yes, it is normal," I said.

I could see the relief in his eyes.

The first year of grief, for me, was extremely difficult. When I looked at the pictures of our happy family, I had to turn away. Why? Because I knew that that family did not exist anymore, and those types of pictures would never happen again. My late wife would never be in new photographs with me again. There would be no new photos of her and the kids. A photograph is a small picture in time but also captures the love and emotions we have for those people.

The love and emotion in a picture can never be duplicated with that loved one again.

Photographs present such a challenge. We take pictures in the good times so we can remember them later. Then when we lose someone, those pictures remind us of what we have lost.

When will I be able to look at them again? I asked myself when I was first widowered.

As I healed, I found that my attitude was changing. I cannot give a timeline of this change because it will be different with each person. But the progression was interesting.

Right after her death, I looked at the photos and cried because they showed me what I had lost: a spouse and good times and family.

Then the pictures brough sadness—I was sad that there would never be times like that again. I was accepting that the loss had happened and that life, the family life in the pictures, would never exist again.

Then the pictures were okay. Yes, okay, because I felt less pain while remembering, and I smiled a little because the pictures were of good times.

Jane, a widowed friend, said she yelled at pictures of her late husband. She was angry at him for dying. After many years, she can now smile at his picture.

Then came the time where I made a conscious decision of what pictures to display. The question was how many and what pictures of my late wife did I want to look at each day, and what about the family? Yes, the new family of the boys and me. We were still a family.

I decided to only have two small pictures of my late wife and me. I put them where I could see them. The pictures on the family wall became those of the boys and me. The three of us were the family. These were our life's memories.

It did not take away or negate their mother's life. We all knew she existed, but she didn't exist for the pictures we put up.

As time went on, a couple of things happened. I decided to sell my house, and I had to depersonalize my house. All the family pictures went into bins to be displayed another day in another house.

Then I remarried. We had a blended family. We had a new house to decorate with our family pictures.

On our wall of family pictures, we put up pictures of our grandparents, us, our parents, siblings, nieces and nephews, kids, and grand kids. We decided not to put up pictures of our previous spouses. We were a new couple and a blended family. Our past spouses where linked to our children but not to our present lives. We wanted the pictures to show the new life we had found in each other.

I am glad my wife and I have a wall of pictures of our parents, children, and grandchildren. They are the memories of our life, and the validation that life goes on as we create memorable times together, caught in frozen images.

After a loss, pictures can be hard to look at, yet as time goes on, the pictures can help us heal by accepting the loss and accepting them as our history. We can reminisce with friends and family about the past times. Our deceased loved ones will never be in our lives again, but their pictures remain to validate our lives.

My late mother always wanted to see pictures of the boys, not just of my boys, her great grandsons as well. The pictures would bring a smile to her face. She could see them, almost as if they were in front of her. The photos helped her to remember them, when she became forgetful and too frail to travel.

Photographs bring nostalgia, and memories that we cannot replace. According to What's Your Grief, images are tangible proof of our loved ones. They remind us of who we were, where we came from, and the people we loved. Memories can get fuzzy after many years. Photos show us the history of our families and how the generations have grown. They also honor the memory and provide a memory of the ones we lost.

Questions

Why did they die?

There are many questions that can be asked about death and dying, bereavement and healing from grief. It is okay to ask questions of ourselves, religious leaders, doctors, counselors, our friends, and even the dead. Children ask 'why' all the time because they want to understand why things are the way they are. We can ask questions too.

Why did they die so young? Why me? Why him? Why her? Why, Lord, why?

Why did they have to die? There are the medical answers of cancer, drug interactions, medical accidents, car accidents, random accidents, murder, or suicide. Yet, there remains the question: 'why' did they have to die that way!

Why did my wife die at the age of 38 and leave me and our two children? I know the medical reasons for her death, but I do not have an answer for why she got cancer or why the cancer could not be eradicated.

There is also the question of why me. Why was I the one that this happened to? Why did I lose my wife? Why did a friend's daughter die? Why did another friend's husband die?

It seems so senseless at times, and makes life seem out of our control too.

I have asked myself 'why' when grief engulfed me and when grief released me. I asked 'why' in anger and in calmness. I screamed 'why' out loud and whispered 'why' in the dark. I yelled 'why' in the car, at the shore, and in the pouring rain. I whispered 'why' to my pillow, to an empty seat, and to anyone who would listen and understand.

We question why our loved one had to go. We question because we do not understand. We want answers. Something to help us understand. Sometimes the answers never come, or the answers are not what we want to hear.

How can we accept that our loved ones had an illness that the doctors, or we, could not cure? How could we not have saved them? How can we accept that our loved one's own actions led to their death? A lifelong smoker may ask why they got lung cancer, but when they think about it, they know why.

I have attempted to answer questions about grief in this book that have plagued and haunted people for years and years. Yet, the question of why someone had to die, beyond the medical diagnosis, is something I do not know. I want to know. I want an answer.

Can religious or spiritual leaders tell us why our loved one died? After my wife died, I heard people say she graduated to a higher plane, her work here was done, she was needed elsewhere, she chose to move on, and other remarks that made an allusion to us having a purpose to our lives—and when that purpose is fulfilled we die.

I was furious with those comments. I needed my wife. Our children needed their mother. Her company, and the medical field, needed her inventions. A father needed his daughter.

"When a loved one passes away, we feel we have lost something precious. We are left with a gaping hole in our heart, and we often wonder why they were taken away from us. But at the same time, we can be grateful for the very fact that they were given to us in the first place. We are blessed to have such beautiful souls in our lives. The world is privileged to have such heavenly guests come down on earth. And even if it can only be for a short while, we will take whatever we can get," said Aaron Ross, rabbi of the Nefesh Community in Sydney, Australia quoted with permission from Chabad.org.

Yes, I am grateful that I had her in my life for twelve years. I am grateful for the children she left me. Grateful for the company to sustain us and provide work for others. Yes, I am grateful for the joy she brought to the world and the light that she was. I can be grateful, but I still want to know why she died.

When we are grieving, we cannot see the millions of people who are grieving the loss of their loved ones too. We cannot feel gratitude that our loved ones were in our lives. Our vision is reduced to our hurting soul. In time, we can see the other hurting souls and care about them. We ask why, oh why did they die? We may never know, but it is okay to ask why and seek help in answering the question.

Rings

What about our rings?

Wedding rings are a symbol of the oath we take on our wedding day. They are a symbol of the love we feel for our spouse. They also become part of our identity as a married couple, committed to each other and to family. Rings have been around for over six thousand years as a symbol of love and eternity. It was a symbol I wore with pride. But what happens when our spouse is no longer with us?

I wore my wedding ring from the day of our wedding onward. I was wearing it when Lisa died. Eight months after Lisa's passing, I was still wearing my ring. At this point, I was sure I was a widower. I accepted that I was not a married man, and I decided it was time to remove my ring. Time to remove the symbol of my marriage and dedication. The decision was not made lightly.

One evening, as I sat in our bedroom staring at my gold wedding band, I did not want to let go of my identity as Lisa's husband. I did not want to accept that our marriage only lasted 8 years. I was plagued with guilt. I had to accept that my wife had died, and I was now single. I had to admit that at age 40, I was a widower with two young children. So here I sat, contemplating removing my ring because I knew that I eventually had to remove my ring.

Yet questions plagued me. If I take the ring off, does that mean I am not loved? Does it mean I do not love Lisa anymore? Does it mean I am a failure? Does it mean I am single when I still feel like I am married? Does it mean I am giving up on the marriage when death ended it?

Without the ring, would people see me as single, never married, or divorced?

I wanted people to know that I had a happy family life and that I kept my wedding vows until death parted us. It was important to me that people knew I took an oath and stuck to it.

I slid the ring off my finger for the first time and felt the cold air spread over the exposed skin of my ring finger. I quickly put the ring back on. The next day I took it off for an hour before returning it to its place.

It is a struggle between wanting to move on and wanting to hang on, between having someone to love and no one to love, and between giving up and giving in.

Two nights later, just before I went to sleep, I took the ring off and placed it on the nightstand. It was close to me but not on me. I slept the night away and, in the morning, I put the ring back on. I survived the night without it.

On the weekend, I again took the ring off, but this time I taped it to a piece a paper and left it on the nightstand and went the whole weekend without wearing the ring. I was stepping out as a new man, a widower, a man alone.

After the weekend without the ring on my finger, I accepted that I could leave it off. It was an acceptance of who I was now. I was willing to accept that I was alone, a single father, and I was alive without my spouse. When I left the house without my wedding ring on, and I had the kids with me, I felt that people were looking at me and assuming I was divorced. They would not think that I was a widower because I was too young.

Several days later, I decided what to do with the ring. I took the ring to the bank for storage in our safe deposit box.

I sat in the small private cubicle and opened the safe deposit box. I reviewed its contents: real estate deeds, cemetery deeds, and a safety pin holding Lisa's engagement ring and her wedding ring. I opened the safety pin and looked at her engagement ring—memories of the time when I proposed to her came flooding back.

It was the day after Thanksgiving, and we were in Vermont, on a ski lift for the first ride up the mountain. The temperature was near freezing. I reached into my puffy down jacket and pulled out the small, black velvet box and handed it to Lisa.

She took the box, put her gloves and ski poles on her lap and opened the box. Her jaw dropped and she looked at me with a puzzled look.

The look on her face was priceless. I was all smiles. And thinking back and feeling the love and happiness that I felt on that day still makes me smile.

"Will you marry me?" I asked.

"Yes," she said.

It was the happiest day of my life and my worst day of skiing.

I pick up her wedding ring—a gold band inset with diamonds. Engraved inside is our wedding date and the initials 'tmwlr,' which means 'to my wife, love Rich.'

We had an evening wedding at our church, and in front of one hundred people, we vowed to be husband and wife 'till death do us part.' We then slid the rings over each other's fingers.

I put her rings back on the safety pin.

The inside of my ring has the date of our marriage and the initials 'tmhll', which means 'to my husband, love Lisa.' I smiled. She loved me and I loved her. I thanked God for giving her and the boys to me.

I took my ring off and slipped it over the open pin, and the ring slid down, coming to rest, against Lisa's ring. I closed the pin, put it into the box and closed the box lid. I sat absorbing another step toward living life without Lisa. It was another step in healing from the hurt after her death. Another step toward adapting to my new life without her.

It was not easy acknowledging her death even after 8 months. It was not easy acknowledging that I had to move on, and not easy removing the symbol of our marriage. Our rings, the symbols of our love, are now together, as I know that Lisa and I will be together again. It is a move I knew I needed to make. I did it.

Could I have left my ring on longer? Yes, I could have. Eight months after Lisa died was my time to remove my ring. Your time could be sooner or later.

There are people who remove their rings and have jewelry made of it, so they are wearing the ring, but not on their finger.

Removing your ring is a step in the healing process. Whether you remove it soon after your spouse dies or later makes no difference. It is your timeline that matters. It is how you feel about it that matters. It is the acceptance that your spouse has died, and an acceptance of your new identity as a single person.

Rings symbolize our love, yet love lives on in our hearts—a place no one can see. People can hear an oath of love, they can see a ring of love, but they cannot see what that means to us. Our rings may be off, but our love lives on.

Sex

Can I have sex again?

Sex is a physical expression with someone we love. Sex is a part of what makes intimate moments intimate. After our loss, having sex is not high on our list of needs. The wounds are deep. Our feelings are scrambled. Our emotions raw. We want our old intimacy back, but cannot find that, at least not immediately. Our bodies feel numb and dead like our feelings.

According to Nicky Gumbel, an English Anglican priest, "…in marriages or long-term relationships, sex is not just physical and biological, but emotional, psychological, spiritual, and social. We express who we are with our bodies in uniting with another person. It is not just the physical that is damaged when being widowed, but part of who we were and how we expressed that spiritual and emotional love."

That sexual urge was diminished by my wife's illness, hospital stays, and medical tests. There was no room for sexual feelings. I was dealing with denial, anger, disbelief, then a funeral and grief. My emotional concerns shut down my body's concerns. I was in survival mode.

Then. Surprise! One day my body signaled that it was ready for sex. How can my body be ready for sex when my mind isn't, and my wife is dead?

For men, an erection is a good thing. It means our blood is flowing and we are alive. It means our body's working. Life is coming back. There is hope. We are still men with physical feelings and reactions. Can our old selves be far behind?

It may seem wrong at the time to have sexual feelings, but it is part of the process men and women go through.

According to Sienna Fein, Blogger, Journalist, Seniors' Sex and Dating Counselor writing in the Huffington Post, "...some men take the inability to get an erection as a sign that they cannot love anymore." The search for a new partner is not without complications, including what Dr. Walter M. Bortz calls "widowers' syndrome."

"It is a classic psychogenic cause of erectile dysfunction in the older male," said Helen Kuno, writing in the book 'Functional Neurobiology of Aging.' "...this can lead to intense feelings of guilt, mainly caused by a feeling that they are being unfaithful to the dead partner.

"Psychogenic refers to a psychological origin rather than a physical one. Guilt about experiencing pleasure without his wife, or even the fear that his deceased wife is 'watching,' has prevented many a man's erection."

I felt guilty the first time I had sex after my wife died. I was feeling guilty that I was cheating on her. Guilty that I had been weak enough to have sex. It was a shock and an eye-opener. I was not married but I still felt like I was. My emotions and spiritual connection were still with my late wife. Through sex, I experienced good physical feelings that were not grief-related, and I needed some good feelings at that time in my life.

We must know whether the inability to get an erection is psychological or physical. Physical problems do increase as men age due to our overall health. Medications, lifestyles, hormone levels and levels of interest, all add up to problems, and a doctor can help sort through what the issue is and what to do.

Do women go through the same thoughts and feelings?

"It's a grief that no one talks about," said neuropsychologist Dr. Alice Radosh in an interview with writer Jane Brody. "But if you can't get past it, it can have negative effects on your physical and emotional health, and you won't be prepared for the next relationship, should an opportunity for one come along."

Dr. Radosh, 75, calls it "sexual bereavement," which she defines as grief associated with losing sexual intimacy with a long-term partner.

It is common for widows and widowers to long for intimacy and sexual relations after losing our loved one. I was looking for that physical intimacy, closeness and caring, that I lost with the death of my wife.

For men, having an erection is a good thing. It is your body telling you, you are alive, and to accept the fact that you are healing. For women, healing can lead to a healthy relation and the love, intimacy, and sex you want. You must be ready for the next relation if it comes along.

Getting back my sexual urge was a shock to me. I did not expect to have those physical reactions again, or so soon. But I am glad it came back. It was a sign that my body and mind were healing. As I worked more on my grief, I knew I would be mentally and physically ready for the relationship.

Men and women can rediscover their sexual drive and enjoy sex again. We must accept that we are single, that our partner is deceased, and that a new sexual relationship is not cheating. Sexual urges are signs that we are healing and that our bodies are ready to participate in a new relationship if we choose to have a new relationship. It is okay to be sexual again. It is your choice.

Sharing widowhood

Who do I share widowhood with?

There are many life experiences that we share with others our own age. Even as young adults, we can share experiences with our parents, even if we never talk about it. There is dating, having children, a house, faith, and the day-to-day struggles of life. One experience that I never thought about sharing was the experience of being a widower with my widowed father-in-law or my widowed mother.

During a normal and typical life cycle, our grandparents and our parents die before us. My grandparents died before any of my siblings or my parents. But not everyone is typical.

When I married Lisa, my father-in-law, Carl, was already a widower, and his only son had been killed in the Vietnam War. All we had in common was his daughter, who was now my wife. My mother and father were still alive, as were my grandmothers.

When Lisa died, Carl and I were now widowers together, separated by 37 years of age. I could now understand what he had gone through before I arrived on the scene. We were now grieving different losses—he a daughter, me a wife, but we were both widowers.

Three years after Lisa died, my father died. Now my mother and I were going through the same experience, separated by 30 years of age.

How could we all relate? In the bereavement group I attended, we talked about the emotions of losing a spouse. The three of us—my mom and Carl and I—shared the loneliness, the longing, and the long nights of fear and uncertainty, but we did not talk about it.

Carl was grieving the death of his daughter; I was grieving the loss of my wife; and my sons were grieving the loss of their mother. My parents were grieving the loss of a daughter-in-law. My siblings were grieving the loss of a sister-in-law. My sister-in-law was grieving the loss of her sister. And on and on it goes with extended members of our family. One loss affects so many relationships.

I had related to Carl as his son-in-law. He and Lisa had their father-and-daughter relationship. We were all adults living together in a large multigenerational household. Lisa had always acted as a go-between. Now it was just him and me, man-to-man. It did not change the way I felt about him. He was someone I had grown to love, respect, and care about.

My mother and I had to relate without my father. Instead of me in a relationship with my parents, it was me in a relation with just my mother. We were longing and missing the same person but from totally different perspectives and relationships. My mother and I got along well because we had a good relationship before my father died.

There was plenty of grief and misery to go around.

Mostly we did keep each other company. For the first two months, we lived together in my house. That was the biggest help to me—to have family around. We were not alone in our grief. We had someone near who understood grief, all its stages and progress, and the person we lost. Even though we were grieving different losses, it was still the loss of a loved one.

Everyone who has lost someone shares grief. Sometimes we must grieve alone, and at other times, we can share the grief with others who are grieving.

I have friends who grieve the death of a child. I know the death of my wife was bad but losing my child would be worse. Yet, we understand the pain that death brought to our lives, and the understanding that we are forever changed.

Yes, widows and widowers understand grief. We cope with it as individuals, but we can be there for each other as we grieve the death of a loved one. We, and they, are our support network. We share a similar experience. We have common ground. We have understanding. We are in a relationship with family sharing a common traumatic event. We help each other by being present.

We are not alone. We can share our grief with widowed parents, in-laws, aunts and uncles, cousins, and siblings. Our relationships, our connections with others who knew our loved one, have changed. We grieve over the same person; yet we grieve as widow to widow, widower to widower. We share a similar experience. We can all help each other because we understand the grieving process.

Single parent

How do I parent as a widower?

"You're the worst father there is," shouted my 12-year-old son.

My son was ranting and raving about the injustices he suffered due to my rules. Rules that I had ranted and raved about when I was his age. I smiled as I saw the similarities. The similarities were in the ranting and raving, not in our upbringing.

I was raised by my mother and father with three other siblings. My son has a sibling, and his mother, my wife, died 7 years ago. I am happy that his rants are normal.

When my wife died, I knew I would never be the same. For one, I had to learn to be the only parent. Meaning there was no backup during the day or night. There was no one to tell stories to and dream about the future of our lives and our children. My late wife and I imagined that we would grow old and gray together, watch the kids grow and mature, and bring us grandchildren. The normal stuff that most married people dream of. That dream ended when my wife was diagnosed with cancer.

It was an aggressive cancer. She fought it for four years, but it never stopped attacking her body. It robbed our kids of their mother and father relationship. It left me as the only parent. I had to step up.

I had been home raising the kids before my wife died. I am a creative type, so making believe a rocking chair was a roller-coaster or crawling through the house was crawling through the woods, were perfectly normal activities for me to do with young kids.

Yet, after my wife died, I felt that I needed more parenting skills to save my sanity, build a healthy relationship with my kids, and to minimize their trauma at losing their mother. Not an easy list but I did find a course called 'Redirecting Children's Behavior.'

This course, developed by Katherine Kvols, gave me tips and strategies that helped me and gave my kids a sense of power and fulfillment. I learned to take the emotion out of disciplining. If I lost my temper, then the kids knew they could get under my skin. I also learned to stick to my guns. I had to enforce rules to ensure that they knew there were rules, and what would happen if they broke them.

I had to follow through on every punishment, choice, and consequence. If I did not follow through, they would walk all over me. I did not want my elementary schoolkids walking all over me because when they became teenagers, they would walk all over me too. That scenario is not good for me or them.

What you do as a parent of elementary school-age kids will have an effect when they are in high school and beyond. Remember to reassure your kids that you are there for them and you are not going anywhere. They need this reassurance. They just lost one parent, and they may think the other could leave too.

When the boys were 8 and 9, they did not want to go to bed at the normal hour, which meant I was not going to get any peace. I instituted a bedtime. I would put them in their room, say goodnight, close the door, and walk away. Of course, they came out. I returned them to the room, closed the door, said goodnight, and walked away. Sometimes I only took one step before they opened the door. Did it work the first night? No.

It was two weeks of me putting them to bed, saying goodnight, walking away, coming back, and closing the door again. Two weeks. No emotions. No discussions. Just saying to them that its bedtime. Did I get angry inside? Yes. Frustrated? Yes. But it worked. After two weeks, they knew that what I said was what I meant. I never had a problem with bedtime after that.

I could not give them their mother relationship, but I gave them my time.

I was there when they left for school and I was there when they returned. I listened to them. It only takes about 60 seconds for an elementary schoolkid to tell you something. If you listen to them now, it will carry on into adulthood. This is active listening, not just casual, but listening to what they say and how they say it. It is your chance to connect with them and build trust and respect.

As a dad, I did 'man stuff' with them. We went to professional ballgames. I went to their ballgames, soccer games, and basketball.

We painted houses, pounded nails, and canoed. But there were situations where I could not do it all or break myself in two. Because I had not remarried, I hired a lady to help me drive the kids around and to give me a break.

Being a widowed parent means being the single parent at school assemblies, or at family day in school—like a divorced parent. The big difference is that there was no other parent to show up. No other parent to tell what happened at school. I could talk to my sister, brother, mother or father, but their relationship with me and the kids is entirely different.

They love them for who they are, but they cannot love them like the flesh and blood of a parent.

When I was with the kids and I met people, the question I was always asked was: 'where is your wife'? That question brought the three of us back to the event that changed our lives.

Being a parent is about the small things that happen every day. At the same time, it is also about what those small things will mean to the kids and me in 20 years. Will I raise sons who will turn into good fathers? Will they laugh and play with their kids? Will they cherish the short time they have together? Will they have patience with their kids when their kids' rail against them?

Will I raise good kids who will treat me well when I and old and frail?

I am older now but not frail as I write this, and the kids are now in their 30s, with kids of their own. They have turned out to be good men, loving sons, and good parents. My parenting is now over, and I am a grandparent. I talk to the grandkids. My wife and I have them sleep over at the house, and we play board games with them or go for a swim.

I now talk to my kids as adults. We are on an equal footing. We share the parenthood experience together.

One night, our seven-year-old grandson was sleeping over. He went to bed but got up after a while. I walked him back to bed. Pulled the cover over him and stroked his hair and said goodnight. This simple act brought me back twenty-five years to when his father was seven.

Twenty-five years ago, I was grieving the loss of his mother. While I was grieving, I could not enjoy this type of simple act. I assume I did it, but I cannot remember my kids at that age. It is very strange and sad. I can look at pictures and see the past, but I have a hard time remembering our interactions during the first couple of years of grieving. That is indeed a pity for me.

There were many days when I was burnt out, I was done, and I wanted to walk away. I needed a break. I think many parents can relate to this. In those times, a sitter or a family member came in so I could go out and do nothing but recharge and be ready to come back.

Love, family, memories, and sharing. All we can do is what we can do as widows or widowers. We raise children and grieve at the same time. We hope our children leave behind the grief of childhood and enter adulthood less scared than when they were kids. We can only hope and pray that it happens.

I have seen my kids grow and go out into the world. I see them as adults. How much the loss of their mother plays in their lives I do not know. We do not talk about that impact, but we are starting to broach the subject. I wonder what effect it had, and I always will. I could only do my best. I made mistakes. I hope they can forgive me for those mistakes and make the best of their lives.

As for my twelve-year-old son ranting and railing against me? Later that evening, he came up to me.

"I love you," he said.

"I love you too," I said, and gave him a hug.

I loved being a father, and still do. It was an emotionally and physically hard job, but the rewards happened every day in small surprises like watching the kids discover their world and their talents.

Being a single parent is hard because of the 24-hour, seven day a week responsibility of our kids. Even when we have help, we are still responsible for them. They are ours to love, cherish and have fun together too.

Spiritual

Do we still have a connection with the deceased?

According to Emilia Gordon, writing in The Mind's Journal, "...a spiritual relationship is when a couple experiences harmony, understanding, and peace. Emotions come from deep within the core or the heart, physically and mentally. There is a feeling of being liberated, you have known them for ages, you trust them, you can communicate in silence, and you can have deep conversations with them."

We strengthen and heal the physical through physical exercise. We heal emotions through grief counseling. It is the spiritual connection, as described above, where I felt the greatest loss, and I had the most difficulty in meeting people and searching for a new partner.

It was the connection I felt with my late wife that told me she was the one. The same was true when I met my second wife.

Now that my first wife is gone, how do I heal the spiritual connection?

"We can begin healing," said Alethcia Luna, an influential spiritual writer, "...by getting in touch with who we are. It can be a journey into who we were before we were married, and finding ourselves." I took this journey after my wife died—to find myself and to find the emotional starting point to allow me to restart my life. It is finding your soul, said Luna.

I knew who I was, but the emotional side of me, as a 40-year-old widower, felt more like a teenager because I was scared and unsure of myself.

You can seek this guidance from therapists, spiritual healers, or clergy. The goal is not to get rid of the feelings you have but to integrate them into your being and feel healed. You are the sum of your experiences and feelings. The Minds Journal website says that "...denying or resisting your feelings does not help you. That is denying part of who you are. Why would you do that? You want to heal, don't you?"

You want to be yourself and get back to the person you were. It is integrating the memories of your late partner and being okay that you are alive. "The way to heal," said Luna, "...is to face the facts, accept them, try to alleviate the suffering, but not to escape the reality, but to love yourself."

This is not easy work. I did not want to admit my wife died, but I had to accept the reality. I did not want to be a single dad, but I had to accept and admit I was. I did not want to accept that I was lonely, needy, pitiful, angry, depressed, and anxious. But I was. When I admitted all of this, I could then work to resolve each issue. As I resolved each issue, I came closer to who I was before my wife died and became more open to accepting others into my life.

As I became more open and accepting, I could see the possibility of a long-term relationship and the liberty that a relationship brings. I wanted the freedom to be me in a relationship again. As I dated, I still made mistakes in being open and accepting, but I knew I was getting closer to being myself and being able to express that. Then it happened. I found a partner to connect with in an emotional, understanding, and spiritual way. It was liberating.

Love is expressed on many different levels. What I was seeking was the spiritual connection where I could be free to be me. Free to love and be loved. Free to express my thoughts, ideas, humor, and still be accepted. I found that.

Relationships take work. If you have the freedom to be you and accepted by your new partner, then you have found a spiritual connection and can live and love in harmony, understanding, and peace.

Stages of grief

Do I have to go through them?

The five stages of grief, as identified by Psychiatrist and author Elizabeth Kubler-Ross, are denial, anger, bargaining, depression, and acceptance. Originally, they were what Kubler-Ross observed in patients receiving a terminal diagnosis. But survivors have also been found to go through stages too.

The stages look like this: There is the denial that anything is wrong. Then anger that it is happening. Then we bargain to make it not happen. Then we are depressed when it does happen. Then we accept that it did or will happen.

The stages do not have to go in order. They can overlap, return, can be skipped over, or only one or some may be felt. There is nothing wrong with experiencing them all or only one. Everyone grieves differently. There is no right way to grieve.

"Studies," says David B. Feldman, Ph.D., author, speaker, and professor of counseling psychology at Santa Clara University, now show that "...the griefstricken do not progress through these stages in a lock-step fashion. Consequently, when any of us loses someone we love, we may find that we fit the stages precisely as Kubler-Ross outlined, or we may skip all but one. We may race through them or drag our feet all the way to acceptance. We may even repeat or add stages that Kubler-Ross never dreamed of. In fact, the actual grief process looks a lot less like a neat set of stages and a lot more like a roller-coaster of emotions. Even Kubler-Ross said that grief does not proceed in a linear and predictable fashion."

I went through these stages when Lisa was diagnosed with cancer and then when she died. I spent a lot of time in denial.

Lisa spent time in denial too. She denied that the cancer was going to kill her. She denied it until the day she died. Whether she came to accept it, was angry, bargained, or was depressed, I never knew. She fought to survive but her feelings were not expressed to me. If they were, I did not hear them.

I denied that she was terminal. Then I accepted that she had cancer, but I still acted like nothing was wrong. My friends told me, years after Lisa died, that they were worried about me because I did not seem to be accepting the inevitable. I did not want to accept the fact that my young wife was going to die. I was in full and total denial, and denial lasted for years as she fought the disease, until I could not deny it any longer. Then I became angry.

Denial is not all bad. It is the brain's way of helping us adjust to grief a little at a time. "Denial becomes unhealthy only when it's unshakeable," said Dr. Feldman.

I went into acceptance when I spoke to both of her doctors and found out how bad her health really was, and that was only weeks before she died. I did not bargain for her life. I accepted that she would die, and that left me depressed. Yet I was calm because I knew there was an end to her suffering.

Jane, a widow, said that the stages came in order, but she did not experience all of them. "I was never in denial that Bob was sick," she said. "Aside from the pain that enfolded me after losing my soul mate, anger set in with a vengeance." Anger is her frequent visitor. Accepting Bob's death took her a long time.

Jane also lost her adult daughter in a car accident. She dealt with all stages of grief during that traumatic time too—including anger. And she focused her anger on the drunk driver that caused her daughter's death. He is now in jail.

I did not go through all the stages that Kubler-Ross identified singularly or in order, or even go through all of them. Each one of us relates to our deceased loved ones differently and that affects which stages we go through, and for how long.

From diagnosis to death, our loved ones go through a range of emotions that can be summed up in the five stages of grief. Those of us left behind also go through stages of grief. We can experience all of them or a few, we can linger in some and rush through others. The stages of emotions at the loss of a loved one are real. We must accept our loss, work through the emotions, and live our lives the best we can.

Stress

How can stress affect my physical health?

Countless studies have proven that stress causes illness, disease and even death. Life is often filled with stress. So, when stress overwhelms you, is a serious illness in your future? Or is there a way to avoid illness, reduce the stress, and get back to living a fulfilling life?

Of course, some stresses take a bigger toll than others. Certainly, losing a job is a high-level stress; divorce is another. But perhaps the ultimate stress one can suffer is the death of a loved one.

According to the *British Medical Journal*, chronic job stress leads to heart disease and diabetes. It has also been proven that the loss of a spouse can be fatal for the spouse left behind. In fact, one study discovered that people rate the death of the spouse as the number one stress of their lifetime. *The New England Journal of Medicine* revealed that the death rate of the spouse accelerated after their other half was merely hospitalized. The risk of death associated with a spouse's hospitalization is higher for men (22%) than women (16%). Not surprisingly, the year following the death of their spouse, the death rate of the surviving spouse spikes significantly.

This is called the 'widower's syndrome' because the surviving spouse cannot live without their other half. It is very poetic, but also deadly serious. Amy Florian, educator, author, public speaker, and Founder/CEO of Corgenius, states "...grief suppresses the immune system, making it more likely for grieving people to get sick, even to the point of extreme stress, resulting in failure of the heart. A broken heart is not just theoretical, it is physical."

When my beloved wife succumbed to cancer, it took the full force of my will merely to get out of bed in the morning. I admit I might have just stayed in bed and "waited for the inevitable," if it were not for my five and six-year-old boys who needed me now more than ever.

I started going to the gym, yet I wound up in the hospital with a heart monitor at age forty-one. Was this the big one? No, it was not. It was stress-related, but stress of my muscle and skeleton system that was causing pain on the left side of my chest—the same left side that I had injured in a moped crash years ago.

My kids were stressed after this event. Their mother had died only a year before and they did not want to lose their dad too. I was lucky.

It could also be that I was young. Florian states that "...couples that have been married for forty years or more are older and may have more health problems than younger people Add to their age the stress of losing a spouse and that could impact their health far more than younger widowers and widows. The most common ailment in older couple is infections."

According to a Pfizer Medical Team article, "...other ways that the death of a loved one can affect your physical health is through alcohol and substance abuse. It is not just for the surviving spouse, but kids too can be at risk for substance and alcohol abuse when they have lost a parent. There is also poor sleep, which can affect your health."

As we work to reduce the stress, try getting a good night's sleep, start to exercise, and socialize with other people—it can reduce stress. Talk to your medical doctor about how to strengthen your immune system. Stress is part of life, but it does not have to kill you. Take precautions and stay well.

Valentine's Day

How do I feel good?

Valentine's Day is the most two-some holiday of the entire year. But what if you have no Valentine, or no significant other? What if your beloved Valentine has died and yet you are besieged with images of Cupids, hearts and love, love, love as Valentine's Day approaches? I know this heartbreak firsthand as my wife died two months before Valentine's Day.

At first, I just wanted to stay in bed and pull the covers over my head because all the images and advertising made it seem that everyone had someone for Valentine's Day, except for me, of course. So, to ease my emotional pain, I needed to find ways to feel better on that day.

From my experience and personal research, I have formulated five tips for getting through Valentine's Day without a valentine. I hope they help you too.

1. Make someone else's day enjoyable. Volunteer at a nursing home or a hospice and hand out valentines, bring cookies to share and make your entire focus about helping someone else feel better.

2. Get physical. Go rock climbing, ride bicycles, go kayaking, work out or take a walk instead! Call a friend or acquaintance, who is also missing their true love, and plan to do something fun together on Valentine's Day. Hint: ignore the romantic restaurant scene.

3. Bring flowers and candy to an elderly person in your neighborhood. Stay for an extended chat and give the gift of listening to your neighbor's stories about her or his life—even if you have heard them many times before. Remember your parents and your adult children on Valentine's Day. Tell them how much you love them and how grateful you are to have them in your life.

4. Throw a Valentine's Day party for little children—your own, your grandchildren, those of your friends and neighbors. Decorate a big box with red and white crepe paper, cut a slot in the cardboard and have the children "mail" their valentines. You could have them make their own valentines at the party and then "mail them" in the decorated box. You can distribute the valentines after you serve cookies and ice cream.

5. Be your own valentine. Treat yourself with love and care. Send yourself flowers. Watch your favorite movie. Read a book in bed. Treat yourself to a special bottle of wine and exquisite cheese. Indulge in a spa treatment—a massage, manicure, pedicure or a facial—which can help you feel good and more

positive about yourself. This "treat yourself" tip is perhaps the most important tip of all.

Valentine's Day without a special someone can feel empty, lonely, and depressing. All those images of love, love, love? Turn it around. Love the person who needs it the most: you. I hope these tips work for you as they have for me. The first time you try these tips, it may seem odd and contrived, but as you use them and mold them to fit your life, they will feel okay. Take care and pamper yourself. Your heart needs healing and love too.

Visiting the past

Do I have to visit the past?

There are many places that you and your deceased loved one may have visited as a couple. You built memories together. Yet, visiting the past is not the same as living in the past. Visiting the past is going to places that you and your loved had gone to. This is where you go to make peace with that part of your life. It is something I did to help me accept my past.

When you are a couple, whether it is a short- or long-term relationship, there are places you go to. Those places become part of your shared memory. It can be a wide range of places from your favorite neighborhood restaurant to trips overseas or picking out what color to paint the kitchen.

And every time you talked about that place, or went there with your loved one, it reinforced the bond between the two of you and that place.

My late wife Lisa and I did that too.

When we traveled, we were building memories not only of that place, but of our marriage, and we were going to relive and share those memories far into the future. The same thing when we traveled with the kids. There was always that certain ice cream stand we went to, or we roasted marshmallows over an open fire with the kids. Sometimes, we even took the kids when we traveled for business. We shared many places with family and friends. Those places are in our memory.

After my wife died, a psychologist friend encouraged me to meet her in Italy. Lisa had only been gone 6 months, and we had visited Italy on our honeymoon. After much internal debate, I went. I did not know what to expect of myself and my reaction to the places Lisa and I had visited. When my friend left, I was alone in Rome. I set out across Rome to find Lisa's spirit in the places we had visited while on our honeymoon.

I visited the places we had been to and spent time at each place. I was looking for her. Well, not the physical her but I was searching for her spirit. I wanted to see if I felt the same way without her as I had with her. In each space I sat, listened, and waited. I remembered the time we were there. I waited until I knew she was not there and there were no ties to that spot. I was alive, a widower, so I left that place satisfied not to have found her.

It was a relief. I now knew that I could be without her in the places we had visited together. According to What's Your Grief website, I learned that I could talk and reminisce about those places without feeling depressed or sad. I had confronted my past and would move on.

The vacation house we owned was different. We had designed the small ranch house and had it built on land she had purchased before we were married. Her spirit and influence were everywhere. Just like separating from personal items, I had to work on what I wanted, and work to make it my own space.

The house was furnished with furniture that had been ours, and new furniture that I bought. I made it a vacation house for me and the kids. But as time went on, we used the house less and less, especially as the boys became teenagers and did not want to go away from their friends. It became another property to maintain. I was busier too and not using it. Instead of letting it sit empty and nagging at me like an old scar, I rented it out on a year-round basis. This way I knew it was in good hands, with someone who would care for it and use it more than I could.

Four years later, the tenant was moving on and asked if I was going to sell it. I had not thought about selling it. Could I part with it? I visited the feeling of the house and my attachment to it, and my new life with my new wife, and I sold the house to a family that was going to build their own memories there. I liked that. All the furniture in there that had belonged to my late wife and me, I moved to a new vacation place closer to my new wife's family. The new owners said we can visit at any time if we want to see the house.

According to 'What's your Grief' website, "...there are many ways to say goodbye to a house. I visited one last time before the sale.

Visiting the old house with new people would seem awkward but the house would be alive again—changed, but alive with new people."

My new wife and I have places we visited in our past too. We do not want to live in the past that has pain associated with it, so we visit places neither of us has visited before. We are building new memories in new places.

There comes a point where you have to make peace with the past. Yes, the past happened. Yes, we have memories of a happy life with someone who is now deceased. Those memories involve places that brought the both of us joy. The memories are just that—memories. We can choose to live in the past and not move forward—and that would create problems in developing new friends and relationships—or we can visit those places of the past and put the past to rest.

According to Edith Moscowitz, entrepreneur, and creator of Vortex-Success. "When you make peace with your past, you create a whole new sense of freedom- freedom from negative vibration, freedom to forgive yourself and others, and the freedom to evolve and actualize your greatest potential."

Living in the moment is living in the present. The past places you visited are what has happened already. You cannot change the places you visited, but you can change how you remember them. You can visit any place you want. It is yours for viewing or building new memories. The past has no hold on you.

Watching a death

What is it like watching someone die?

"Being with someone you love when they die is a profound experience," says the website Dying Matters in their post on being with someone when they die. "Nonetheless, you may find the anticipation emotionally and mentally exhausting. At times, you may fervently wish for it to be over. And then you may feel guilty for thinking like this." But it is a normal and understandable response to an incredibly stressful situation, Dying Matters says.

I watched my wife die. I was 39, and she was 38. After 3 years of battling cancer she went into the hospital and two months later she slipped into a coma on a Saturday, and she died on Monday.

When I arrived at the hospital the day she slipped into the coma, she was breathing but she was not able to look at me or respond to my voice. She was just staring at the ceiling and breathing. She did not respond to the voices of family and friends that came to visit over the weekend.

Monday afternoon, after her doctor and I discussed a 'Do Not Resuscitate' order, her breathing changed from steady to ragged, I knew that was not a good sign. But I did not know when she would pass. Over a 12-hour period I heard and watched her breathing become more ragged and then slow down. I talked to her and held her hand. But there was still no response or recognition from her that I was there.

I felt her hand tighten around mine. She exhaled her breath and her hand relaxed. She passed with a breath and a squeeze of the hand.

It was calm and quiet in the hospital room. There was no flailing of limbs or crying out, no last wishes spoken. Just the body relaxing and stopping its function.

I cried when she passed, and I went into shock.

She just lay there like before; except she was not breathing. It was just a body. Her eyes were still fixed on the ceiling. In about an hour, her facial skin became cold to the touch.

I saw another person die. Diseases had ravaged the body and they just stopped breathing too. Quietly they stopped breathing and their life ended. Again, the deceased seemed at peace. The family who were there were relieved—relieved that their loved one's suffering had passed—and saddened at the same time.

Many people, me included, feel that hearing is the last organ to fail, so we talk to our loved one. I talked to Lisa even when she was in a coma, in the hopes that she would know that I was there, and that our friends where there and that she was not alone.

There are no right or wrong feelings when someone dies. When my wife passed, I felt sadness, exhaustion, and guilt. Others feel relief that their loved one is not suffering. They feel a burden has been lifted off them.

Expressing those feelings is neither right nor wrong. They are your feelings.

Being with someone when they die can be an honor. It is also a stressful experience as you watch the last breath and the person you knew ceases to exist. Relief that suffering is over, grief at the loss, being emotionally and physical spent, are not uncommon emotions and feelings to have. Each person is unique in their feelings as is the person who is dying.

We to Me

How do I move from 'we' to 'me'?

It is so natural when we are married to say, 'we did this', or 'we did that', because we did do this, or that, together as a couple. Then when we are widowed, there is no 'we' anymore. How do we get from the married 'We' to the singular 'Me'?

With practice.

Yes, with practice. I practiced saying that because as a young widower, at only 40, I knew that someday I wanted to get married again. I did not know what day, what year, or how old I would be, but I wanted to marry again.

I had to practice saying 'I' did something, instead of 'we' did something. I had to hear myself say that it was 'I' who did something. It was a deliberate choice to say 'me' to make my mind reflect my single existence. It was not easy at first, and one reason is that it cut out the person who I lived my life with.

I found this switch important in general conversations about my past life, and in dating. When I was talking to a new person and they would say 'I did this' or 'I did something', I found it hard to respond as 'I', especially if it was an experience that I had had with my late wife. It was 'we'—my late wife and I—who did the event together. But if I kept using 'we,' then my late wife would always be in the conversation, and my date would accuse me of not moving on. Which would be true. I could not move on or acknowledge my current state of being single, or widowered, if it was always 'we' who did things. I would bc stuck in the past.

Not stuck in a bad way. Widowhood is a transitional state of being and using new terms to describe us is important. Some days, I did not want to move on. Some days, I wanted to move backward. But life goes forward. I did not want to forget what my late wife and I had done together. Yet, I was moving away from the memories we had built. I just wanted to move away from my departed wife as part of the conversation.

If possible, I would have stayed married to her. But life did not work out that way for us. I was left by myself. For me to have someone in my life again, I had to be the singular person—like I was before marriage. That singular person at my age, which was 45 and older, has a history and baggage including children, in-laws, and a late wife. This includes the memories of all my past relationship.

I knew that the person who wanted to be with me would find out about my late wife. I cannot keep that a secret. I have the children to prove it. But I wanted the new woman in my life to realize that I would be in a relation only with her, and not the ghost of my late wife.

There are always dating questions like where did you grow up, why do you have kids and where is the mother? Those hints that you have lived before. There is a certain amount of acceptance of past relationship when you are past the age of forty. Most people do not expect to meet a man, or a woman, who has lost a spouse at a young age. The news that I was married before always came up in the conversation because it is a dating question.

"When dating, the new date will pay attention to your emotional availability and watch for red flags," says Bobbi Palmer, teacher, consultant, manager, and widow. "Are you able to be present? Is your life in the here and now? But these are issues people look for in every case with *every* person they are dating, including you."

At first, I had to stop and think about the pronoun. When talking about travel with someone new, they would say they had been to a certain place that I had also been to, I would switch from we—Lisa and I—and instead say that I had been there. Then I would relate my impressions, thoughts and memories, the singular perspective, and not the shared experience of a formally married person.

I had the experience, remembered it, and now I had to talk about it from my perspective. I did not talk about how my late wife and I shared the experience. Even in our marriage, our shared experiences are seen through our own eyes.

When I remember dating as a teenager, the switch in pronoun use was easy. There were places or events that I did with someone or with a group of friends or by myself. I related my experiences and impressions first, then my past dating history. And some of those dates, I wish I could forget, but dating is trying to find the perfect mate.

As young people, we simply went out, learned about the other person and ourselves, and if it did not work, we moved on to the next person. There was nothing bad about having dated someone before unless you made a reputation that you do not want. It was simply dating.

Dating as a widow, or widower, we have so much experience behind us, yet dating seems odd. It is odd because we have someone to compare our date to, and we shouldn't compare our dates to our late spouses. We still want to find the love of our life, or the next love of our life. I wanted to. Don't you?

My dates were looking for a single person who could commit to them. That was it. I had to be me. I had to be single. I had to live a life that was not anchored or centered on my late wife. I could have memories, but I had to show that I was able and willing to move on and be present. I had to show my date that I was available, both physically and emotionally.

"What woman would not want a man that has been in a committed relationship?" asked Palmer. She says "a widower probably knows how to love, communicate, commit, work through problems and misses being married. The same can be said for widowers who are looking to remarry."

I was getting ready, and I could cook and clean.

After many years of dating, I learned to be open, and when I found the right woman. I was ready. We had to accept our pasts. For me, that meant accepting her ex-husband, as he was still around and part of his daughter's life, even though contact with him was limited. On the other hand, she had to accept that I had a deceased wife, and two grown sons.

She had her baggage. I had mine. We accepted each other's baggage. We were emotionally and physically available to be present with each other. As we dated, I could say 'we' again, because we were building a new life based on a shared vision of the future and our values. We became engaged and got married. We traveled, and yes, we visited this place and that place.

Moving from 'we' to 'me' is not easy. Your mind must accept the reality of being single. You are a single person with a history, but you do not have to live in the past. A new partner will want you to live with them in the present.

You must live in the present. Be available. Find a partner that accepts your past and accepts that you are working on or moving forward. Accept their past too. When you find the right person, hang on and work together to be a couple and enjoy using the term 'we' again.

Epilogue

It is going to be *Okay.* Death, dying, and grief are not easy topics to talk about. Sometimes we do not talk about them until we experience them. Then we are grieving and do not want to talk about it, do not know how to talk about it, and do not know whom to talk to about it.

Sometimes we sit in quiet agony. You know the times when you cannot get out of your own way or do not know who would listen to you? Someone is available to listen to you, and you will be okay.

Grief counselors, in private practice, groups, or in hospices, know how to listen and know how to talk about what is on your mind. They listen to you and affirm what you are going through, feeling, and progressing through. Sometimes sitting in silence is affirmation that you are grieving and alive.

The following words are from singer songwriter Danny Cokey's Song, *Tell your heart to beat again.*

Words fall short at times like these,
Let the shadows fall away,
Yesterday is a closing door,

You do not live there anymore,

Tell your heart to beat again.

These words, though not in the order he sings them, remind me that death opens a door to grief, and grief is an emotion that needs to be felt, then recede into our past. A door closes on our old life but another one opens to our new life so our heart can love, and we can live again.

Yes, life is going to be okay, really. I made it through grief, lived, and remarried, and am enjoying life again. As you work through grief, face it, accept it, and adapt to your new life. You will learn to live again. You will learn to love again. Where you take your life is in your hands, and that is something to look forward too.

You will be okay.

About the Author

Richard Ballo was married to the late Melissa Johnson (1955-1993). Ms. Johnson was the inventor of Cath-Secure and the founder of the M.C. Johnson Co., a medical device company. They were married from 1986 until her death in 1993. He is now married to Terri.

Richard has had more close encounters with death, dying and grieving since Lisa's death. His dad died in 1997. Lisa's dad died in 2005. A past girlfriend was killed in a motorcycle accident. A broken engagement followed. But marriage did follow that. Then his second father-in-law passed, then his mother in 2020.

Richard's books: *Life without Lisa, The Heart of Grief Relief Journal*, and *Bullets and Babies* have all won awards. He is a popular national speaker on the topic of grief and recovery, and helps many with his wisdom, experience and his ability to share what he went through. He has spoken at hospices, churches, public libraries, community centers, clubs, organizations, and bookstores all over the United States.

Richard has appeared as a guest on hundreds of radio talk shows across the U.S. and over 100 articles have been written about him and his work has appeared in newspapers and magazines nationwide.

He has written general interest articles that appeared in numerous newspapers, including *The Montachusett Times, the Sentinel and Enterprise* in Fitchburg, MA, and magazines including *Resource Recycling, BMW ON Magazine*, and *Neapolitan Family*, and several online articles on grief and healing with some appearing on the Open to Hope website.

He is a past Board member at Avow Hospice in Naples, FL., past Trustee of Seacrest Country Day School's Board of Trustees; he is active with Kiwanis, and is a charter member of the Kiwanis Club of Greater Collier, and the Florida Drowning Prevention Foundation. He supports the Harry Chapin Food Bank and The Greater Boston Food Bank, and other civic organizations in his community.

He is the writer and creator of the 'Martin the Mouse' picture book series.

Twenty years after losing Lisa, he met Terri. They are now married and living happily ever after in Southwest Florida. Together, they have a blended family of three grown children and four grandsons.

Other books by Richard Ballo

Martin the Mouse book series:

Richard's books are available at Tolman Main Press, Bookch.com, and Barnes and Nobles' websites. Please visit Richardballo.com, tolmanmainpress.com, or LittleMousePress.com.

References

1. American Psychological Association. (2015). Controlling Anger before it controls you. Retrieved from http://www.apa.org/topics/anger/control.aspx
2. Bagha, M. (2015). 28 normal things by Mounia Bagha, Elite Daily, Retrieved from http://elitedaily.com/life/signs-youre-living-normal-life/1031151/
3. Brody, J.E. (2017). When a Partner Dies, Grieving the Loss of Sex. Retrieved from https://www.nytimes.com/2017/03/06/well/when-a-partner-dies-grieving-the-loss-of-sex.html
4. CDC. (2020). Deaths and Mortality. Retrieved from https://www.cdc.gov/nchs/fastats/deaths.htm.
5. Cokey, D. (2020). Tell Your Heart to Beat Again. Retrieved from https://www.dannygokey.com/. Song at https://www.youtube.com/watch
6. Cort, S. (2010). Helpful advice for Blended Families. Psychology Today. January 6, 2010. Retrieved from https://www.psychologytoday.com/blog/the-power-perspective/201001/helpful-advice-blended-families
7. Dignity Funerals. (n.d.). Types of Memorials. Retrieved from https://www.dignityfunerals.co.uk/memorials/types-of-memorials/
8. Dying matters. (n.d). Being with someone when they die. Dying Matters. Retrieved from http://dyingmatters.org/page/being-someone-when-they die
9. eHarmony. (2016). Intimacy Issues: 4 Must-Tackle Topics That May Scare you. Retrieved from http://www.eharmony.com/dating-advice/relationships/intimacy-issues-4-must-tackle-topics-that-may-scare-you

10. Family Education. (n.d.). The Second Marriage: Building New Memories. Retrieved from http://life.familyeducation.com/marriage/relationships/45620.html
11. Feldman, D. (2019). Why The Five Stages of Grief Are Wrong. Psychology Today. Retrieved from https://www.psychologytoday.com/us/blog/super-survivors/201707/why-the-five-stages-grief-are-wrong
12. Fein, S. J. (2017). Sex and the Grieving Widower. Retrieved from Huffpost.com/Entry/Sex-and-the-grieving-widower.
13. Florian, A. (6.25.2018). Broken Heart Syndrome: Illness After Loss. Retrieved from https://www.nextavenue.org/broken-heart-syndrome/
14. Fritscher, L. (2015). Fear of Intimacy: Understanding the Deeper Issues. About Health. Retrieved from http://phobias.about.com/od/phobiaslist/a/Fear-Of-Intimacy.htmFuneral Guide
15. Gordon, L.H. (1969). Intimacy: The Art of Relationships. Psychology Today. 12.31.1969, reviewed 8.30.2004. https://www.psychologytoday.com/articles/199309/intimacy-the-art-relationships
16. Good Funeral Guide. (n.d.). Retrieved from https://www.goodfuneralguide.co.uk/tombstones-and-ashes/marking-the-spot/
17. Grief Counseling. (n.d.). Anniversary Reactions. Retrieved from https://griefcounselor.org/anniversary-reactions/
18. Chapman, C. (2017). A Psychotherapist in Paris. With Grief, Depression And Losses, Setbacks Are Inevitable. Retrieved from https://www.cherry-chapman.com/2017/07/04/grief-depression-losses-setbacks-inevitable/
19. Gumbel, N. (1996). Is there anything Wrong with Sex Before Marriage. Searching Issues. Page 42.
20. Gunn, A. 2015. Counseling Successful Blended Families. Retrieved from https://minds.wisconsin.edu/bitstream/handle/1793/74130/Gunn%20Amy.pdf?sequence=1
21. Harra, C. (2013). The 10 elements of a soul mate. Soul mate or life partner? 10 elements of a soul mate. Rebelle Society. Retrieved from http://www.rebellesociety.com/2013/10/21/soulmate-or-life-partner/

22. Haley, E. (n.d.). What they meant to say: looking beyond hurtful comments in Grief. Retrieved from https://whatsyourgrief.com/hurtful-comments-in-grief/

23. Harley, F.J. (2015). Why should a Couple Plan to Be with Each Other When They are the Happiest? Marriage Builders. Retrieved from http://marriagebuilders.com/graphic/mbi5069_qa.html

24. Horsley, G. (2015). Open to Hope. Reinvesting in Living After the Loss of A Loved One. Retrieved from https://www.opentohope.com/reinvesting-in-living-after-the-loss-of-a-loved-one/

25. Jacks, D. (2004). Guide to Grief: How to Help Someone Who is Bereaved. Life without Lisa. Second printing, pages 200-204. Here to There, Grief to Peace, (2005).

26. Kubler-Ross, E. (1969). Shock Stage. On Death and Dying. Retrieved from http://changingminds.org/disciplines/change_management/kubler_ross/shock_stage.htm

27. Biography. (n.d.). Retrieved from https://www.biography.com/scientist/elisabeth-kubler-ross

28. Kuno, H., Godschalk, M., Mulligan, T. (2001). Functional Neurobiology of Aging. 51 - Male Sexual Behavior during Aging, Editor(s): PATRICK R. HOF, CHARLES V. MOBBS, Academic Press 2001, Pages 739-747, ISBN 9780123518309, https://doi.org/10.1016/B978-012351830-9/50053-6. (http://www.sciencedirect.com/science/article/pii/B9780123518309500536)

29. Kvols, K. (2019). Redirecting Children's Behavior.

30. Kalish, N. (2011). Late-Life Marriages: The Second (or third) time Around. Psychology Today. https://www.psychologytoday.com/us/blog/sticky-bonds/201111/late-life-remarriages-the-second-or-third-time-around

31. Lamia, M.C. (2011). Grief isn't Something to Get Over. Psychology Today. Posted May 01, 2011. Retrieved from https://www.psychologytoday.com/blog/intense-emotions-and-strong-feelings/201105/grief-isnt-something-get-over

32. Livingston, K. (2014). Growing number of Dads' home with the Kids. Pew Research Center. Retrieved from http://www.pewsocialtrends.org/2014/06/05/growing-number-of-dads-home-with-the-kids/

33. Long, E. (2015). GoodTherapy, 4 Things You Need to Know about 'Moving On' from Grief. Retrieved from https://www.goodtherapy.org/blog/4-things-you-need-to-know-about-moving-on-from-grief-0623155

34. Luna, A. (n.d.). 5 Types of Spiritual Healing. Retrieved from: https://lonerwolf.com/spiritual-healing/. March 31, 2020

35. Maisel, E. R. (Nov 15, 2011). What Do We Mean by 'Normal'? It is time to rethink 'normal' and 'abnormal'. Psychology Today. Retrieved from https://www.psychologytoday.com/blog/rethinking-psychology/201111/what-do-we-mean-normal

36. Mendoza, Dr. M. (2019). Dreams and Grief. Psychology Today. Retrieved from https://www.psychologytoday.com/us/blog/understanding-grief/201904/dreams-and-grief

37. Meyers, S. (2013). Fear of Intimacy in Men: Cause, Relationship Problems, Tips. Psychology Today. Retrieved from https://www.psychologytoday.com/blog/insight-is-2020/201304/fear-intimacy-in-men-cause-relationship-problems-tips

38. Milbrand, L. (n.d). How to Talk to Kids About Death, Step by Step. Parents. Retrieved from https://www.parents.com/toddlers-preschoolers/development/social/talking-to-kids-about-death/

39. Moss, A. (n.d.). Chabad.org. Why do Some of the Best Die Young. Chadad.org. Retrieved from https://www.chabad.org/library/article_cdo/aid/1388654/jewish/Why-Do-Some-of-the-Best-Die-Young.htm. Copyright by the author and Chabad.org, reprinted with permission

40. The Minds Journal. (n.d.). 7 Signs you are spiritual connected with Someone. Retrieved from https://themindsjournal.com/7-signs-you-are-spiritually-connected-with-someone/ 3/30/2020

41. Morrow, A. (2020). Levels of Hospice Care as Defined by Medicare. Verywellhealth.com. Retrieved from https://www.verywellhealth.com/levels-of-hospice-care-1132297

42. Moscowitz, E. (n.d.). How To Make Peace With Your Past: 8 Steps To Letting Go. Vortex Success. Retrieved from https://www.vortex-success.com/about-us/

43. Nader, K. (2014). Gifts from within - PTSD Resources for survivors and caregivers. Retrieved from http://www.giftfromwithin.org/html/Guilt-Following-Traumatic-Events.html

44. National At-Home Dad Network. (2020). What is an "At-Home Dad"? Retrieved from https://www.athomedad.org/about/what-is-an-at-home-dad/

45. Olsen, A. (n.d.). Brainy Quote. Retrieved from http://www.brainyquote.com/quotes/quotes/a/ashleyolse427337.html?src=t_normal_life

46. Palmer, B. (n.d.). Dating a Widower:4 Tips to Make it a Success. Date Like a Grownup. Retrieved from https://datelikeagrownup.com/dating-a-widower-5-tips-to-make-it-a-success/

47. Pavlina, S. (2005). How to Decide When to End a Long-term Relationship. Steve Pavlina.com. Retrieved from http://www.stevepavlina.com/blog/2005/08/how-to-decide-when-to-end-a-long-term-relationship/

48. Pennebaker, J. (2019). https://www.journaling.com/articles/expressive-writing-a-tool-for-transformation-with-dr-james-pennebaker-ph-d/

49. Pfizer Medical Team. (2018). 5 Ways Grief May Affect Your Health. Retrieved from https://www.gethealthystayhealthy.com/articles/5-ways-grief-may-affect-your-health

50. Rhodan, M. (2013). Study: 'House Husbands' More Common Than Ever. Time. Retrieved from http://nation.time.com/2013/09/18/study-house-husbands-more-common-than-ever/

51. Robertson, B. (n.d.). Visitation Dreams: How to Know For Sure If They Are Real. Retrieved from http://blairrobertson.com/blog/visitation-dreams-real-imagined/

52. Schwartz, P. (2015). Starting Over After Losing a Partner. AARP Website. Retrieved from http://www.aarp.org/relationships/love-sex/info-01-2012/advice_for_the_newly_single.html

53. Serani, D. (2016). The Do's and Don'ts of Talking with a Child about Death. Retrieved from https://www.psychologytoday.com/us/blog/two-takes-depression/201612/the-dos-and-donts-talking-child-about-death

54. Tripp, P.D. (2010). Grief: Finding Hope in the Darkness. Familylife. Retrieved from http://www.familylife.com/articles/topics/life-issues/challenges/mental-and-emotional-issues/grief-finding-hope-in-the-darkness

55. Tidd, C. (2011). Maintaining Friendships after A Spouse-loss. Open to Hope. June 28, 2011. Retrieved from http://www.opentohope.com/maintaining-friendships-after-a-spouse-loss/

56. Schwiebert, P. (n.d.). Grief Triggers. Grief Watch. Retrieved from https://www.griefwatch.com/grief-triggers

57. Weiss, J.P. (2015). Three Reasons You Need to visit a Graveyard. The Good Men Project. Retrieved from https://goodmenproject.com/featured-content/three-reasons-you-need-to-visit-a-graveyard-hesaid/

58. Winokuer, H. (2015). Open to Hope. Reinvesting in Living After the Loss of A Loved One. Retrieved from https://www.opentohope.com/reinvesting-in-living-after-the-loss-of-a-loved-one/

59. Wheeler, J. (2015). Testimonial for the Heart of Grief Relief Journal.

60. What's Your Grief. (n.d). What's Your Grief? Sorting Through Belongings. Retrieved from https://whatsyourgrief.com/sorting-through-belongings/

61. What's Your Grief. (n.d.). Saying Goodbye to a Home and Grieving Places Past. Retrieved from https://whatsyourgrief.com/saying-goodbye-to-a-home/

62. What's Your Grief. (n.d.). Survivors guilt. Retrieved from https://whatsyourgrief.com/understanding-survivor-guilt/

Finding Our Way Back

AWARD WINNING AUTHOR

RICHARD BALLO, BS, MBA

Excerpt from Chapter 1

Chapter One

ZERO DEGREES:

The Normal life

Zero degrees, or normal life, is just a name I put on life, at any point in life, because it is life. That means, wherever you are is your normal, zero-degree life, and that includes all past life events. Those events make you, you.

We all have different family dynamics, relatives, cultural backgrounds, and neighborhood interactions. Normal is what we grow up with and are used to. It is also the here and now.

For instance, high school, for me, was a simple time in my life compared to my adult life. I was worrying about my grades and girlfriends. The term 'normal' changes as we age and our life changes.

As Mounia Bagha, a writer, said in an *Elite Daily* post: "It's not like there's a list with a bunch of bullet points we can follow if our sole life ambition is to be labeled as a "normal" human being. And what if the way you live your life actually seems pretty normal to you?"

Each of us is normal in the confines of our own life and our family. Many celebrities, such as Ashley Olsen, know that the world they inhabit isn't completely normal, or like most peoples' lives.

Olsen said, and quoted from Brainy Quotes website, "I live a normal life. I have friends, and I've always gone to school. The part that's not normal is that I've been working since I was 9 months old, but at the same time, it's completely normal to me."

Even psychologists have concerns over what the terms 'normal' and 'abnormal' mean, states Eric Maisel, a psychotherapist and author, on the Psychology Today website.

For this book, the term 'normal life', or the zero-degree point, is the life you are living now, today, in a relationship. It is as simple as that.

Then there is typical or common life. That is what most people of a certain age are doing at or around the same time. High school graduation is typical for most kids. College, work, and career are typical yet different for everyone. Getting a driver's license is typical for most young people. Having a brand-new car as a teenager is not typical in most communities but can be typical in some other communities.

Normal for me, in my 20s, was working two jobs to make ends meet—and sometimes, the ends did not meet. I imagine other people may have gone through similar events or life patterns. I felt like a failure. Yet, I kept working toward something even if I could not see it. That is also typical or normal for some people.

I belonged to a large group of single friends too. Each month the typical thing to do was to go to my friend Joe's house for a dinner party. Each person or a couple of people would cook or buy dinner for the rest of the crowd.

On one typical feast night, I walked into Joe's house, and my friend Carol was sitting at the kitchen table with a brown-haired woman I had never met before. There was no telling who you would meet.

I sat across from the brown-haired woman, and Carol introduced me to Lisa. I looked into Lisa's eyes and saw confidence and strength. What I was feeling and reacting to was what Dr. Carmen Harra cites as a soulmate moment.

Dr. Harra, psychologist and author, further states that "there are no words or explanations that can clearly articulate such a connection. It is a magnetic energy, an intuitive knowing and it just seems right. There is no matter of space or time, you have found your way to one another."

When I look back, I realize it was one of those aha moments. Yet at that point in time all I knew was that I wanted to know her better.

Lisa and I started to date casually. Over the next year, we became known as a couple. This seemed normal to us, but strange to our friends.

She worked her job, and I worked my job, and on the weekends, we started to remodel a house for fun and profit. It was a common interest we both had.

After being a couple for a couple of years, Lisa said we should get more serious or see other people.

Being a typical guy, I had the typical 'deer caught in the headlights' look. In my mind, I was with her, and that meant I wanted to be with her. What does she mean? I thought. So typically, I said nothing, but I started to think about what she had asked, what did she mean, and what my response should be.

"There are many ways to respond, and one typical response to an ultimatum in a relationship is to weigh the pros and cons of staying versus leaving," said Steve Pavlina on his website. I didn't question that I wanted to stay with Lisa, but I started to look at my life. I was comparing how I felt about past relationships that I thought had been good. But did I want to go back to any of them?

The answer was no. I did not want to go back to those past relationships. It came down to Lisa: who she was, how we got along, our shared vision of the future, and how I felt in her presence. I wanted to go forward in a relationship with her. I knew what my answer had to be.

Psychotherapist Mira Kirshenbaum said, in a post by Steve Pavlina, that "...long-term *happiness* is the key criteria used, meaning the happiness of the individual making the stay-or-leave decision, is the key."

I was happy with Lisa. I was happy with the decision I made to stay. I just had to tell her in my own way. My own way was normal and typical for me, but it was probably not normal or typical for anyone else. I decided to stay and ask her to marry me. Was I scared? Yes and no.

Asking is the hardest part but I felt deep down she would say yes. I mean, at this point she was still dating me, and we were moving forward as a couple.

I wanted to propose in a manner that would make a great story we could tell our grandchildren. Yes, grandchildren. This was a lifetime decision I was making. I could see, hear, and feel the future with her.

Some men propose at restaurants with dinner, champagne, and candlelight, which they see as normal, typical and totally romantic. I get that. Other men see it differently. Whatever way men propose, it is typical and normal for them. If she says yes, then it was the right way. I would ask Lisa on a day that had personal meaning for us.

Three months after making my decision to ask her to marry me, I was ready to propose. Our typical winter sport, as we lived in New England, was skiing. It was now November, and we were beginning the year's ski season. On the first day of skiing, on the first chairlift ride up the mountain, I pulled the little black box from the inside pocket of my down jacket and handed it to her. When she opened the box, her jaw dropped, and she looked a little confused, but she did say 'yes'.

It was the best day of my life.

It was my worst day of skiing.

Even though marriage wasn't the answer she had been looking for, it did answer her question of how I felt. We were married three months later.

We became a typical two career family. Three years into our marriage, we had two sons. Life was good. Our kids were in daycare with a friend of ours who was home raising her kids.

Two years later, during a discussion of our kids and our future, I decided to become the stay-at-home parent.

This decision was, and still is, not the typical and normal thing for a husband to do. Journalist Maya Rhodan found that only 22% of stay-at-home dads are primary caregivers, while the rest are disabled, sick or unable to find employment.

I was also younger than the average stay-at-home dads and more educated than my wife. It was right for us, so it was our normal. Stay-at-home dads only numbered around 1 million in back in 1989, and 2 million in 2014 states the National At-Home Dad Network.

Researcher Gretchen Livingston found that most stay at home dads were either ill or fired from a job. I was neither ill nor fired. I took this on myself.

I quit the corporate job and came home. Being home was the hardest job I ever had.

One year later, I finished getting the boys into bed with the typical bedtime routine of stories, back massages, and one more trip to the bathroom or a drink of water. I finally got back to our bedroom.

Lisa was standing near the full-length mirror. She had her hand on her abdomen and said she felt a hard spot. She looked worried and that was not typical for her.

Lisa was a nurse by trade, so if this hard spot was concerning to her, then it was concerning to me. I didn't know what to say or do, so I let her lead the way. That lead to her doctor.

A few weeks later, it was Lisa's 35th birthday. We would have loved to celebrate it in the typical adult way by having a nice dinner and drinks, and then having cake with the kids.

This birthday was not typical.

Lisa was sitting upright in a hospital bed, and I was sitting in a chair next to her hospital bed. We were in the same hospital where she had worked as a nurse, and where the kids were born. We were waiting for the doctor, which is typical. They had run tests, and we were waiting.

Then, the doctor came in.